AF759995

Between growth and security

MANCHESTER
1824

Manchester University Press

Critical Labour Movement Studies

Series editors
John Callaghan
Steven Fielding
Steve Ludlam

Already published in the series

John Callaghan, Steven Fielding and Steve Ludlam (eds), *Interpreting the Labour Party: approaches to Labour politics and history*

Dianne Hayter, *Fightback! Labour's traditional right in the 1970s and 1980s*

Jonas Hinnfors, *Reinterpreting social democracy: a history of stability in the British Labour Party and Swedish Social Democratic Party*

Jeremy Nuttall, *Psychological socialism: the Labour Party and qualities of mind and character, 1931 to the present*

Declan McHugh, *Labour in the city: the development of the Labour Party in Manchester, 1918–31*

Between growth and security

Swedish social democracy from a strong society to a third way

Jenny Andersson

Translated by
Mireille L. Key

Manchester University Press
Manchester and New York
distributed exclusively in the USA by Palgrave

Copyright © Jenny Andersson 2006

The right of Jenny Andersson to be identified as the author of this work has been asserted by her in accordance with the Copyright, Designs and Patents Act 1988.

Published by Manchester University Press
Oxford Road, Manchester M13 9NR, UK
and Room 400, 175 Fifth Avenue, New York, NY 10010, USA
www.manchesteruniversitypress.co.uk

Distributed exclusively in the USA by
Palgrave, 175 Fifth Avenue, New York,
NY 10010, USA

Distributed exclusively in Canada by
UBC Press, University of British Columbia, 2029 West Mall,
Vancouver, BC, Canada V6T 1Z2

British Library Cataloguing-in-Publication Data
A catalogue record for this book is available from the British Library

Library of Congress Cataloging-in-Publication Data applied for

ISBN 0 7190 7439 8 *hardback*
EAN 978 0 7190 7439 4

First published 2006

15 14 13 12 11 10 09 08 07 06 10 9 8 7 6 5 4 3 2 1

Typeset
by Action Publishing Technology Ltd, Gloucester
Printed and bound in Great Britain
by Cromwell Press, Trowbridge, Wiltshire

Contents

Series editors' foreword

The start of the twenty-first century is superficially an inauspicious time to study labour movements. Political parties once associated with the working class have seemingly embraced capitalism. The trade unions with which these parties were once linked have suffered near-fatal reverses. The industrial proletariat looks both divided and in rapid decline. The development of multi-level governance, prompted by 'globalisation' has furthermore apparently destroyed the institutional context for advancing the labour 'interest'. Many consequently now look on terms such as 'working class', 'socialism' and 'the labour movement' as politically and historically redundant.

The purpose of this series is to give a platform to those students of labour movements who challenge, or develop, established ways of thinking and so demonstrate the continued vitality of the subject and the work of those interested in it. For despite appearances, many social democratic parties remain important competitors for national office and proffer distinctive programmes. Unions still impede the free flow of 'market forces'. If workers are a more diverse body and have exchanged blue collars for white, insecurity remains an everyday problem. The new institutional and global context is moreover as much of an opportunity as a threat. Yet, it cannot be doubted that compared with the immediate post-1945 period, at the beginning of the new millennium, what many still refer to as the 'labour movement' is much less influential. Whether this should be considered a time of retreat or reconfiguration is unclear – and a question the series aims to clarify

The series will not only give a voice to studies of particular national bodies but will also promote comparative works that contrast experiences across time and geography. This entails taking due account of the political, economic and cultural settings in which labour movements have operated. In particular this involves taking the past seriously as a way of understanding the present as well as utilising sympathetic approaches drawn from sociology, economics and elsewhere.

John Callaghan
Steven Fielding
Steve Ludlam

Acknowledgements

This book was first published in Swedish as the result of a doctoral thesis, and I want to thank all those who have read and commented on the Swedish publication in the two years following its publication. I am grateful to three reviewers in Sweden, Bo Stråth, Urban Lundberg and Ann-Marie Lindgren, as well as two anonymous reviewers at Manchester University Press. Thanks to a long row of social democrats and policymakers in Sweden who have met and talked to me. I am especially grateful to Ingvar Carlsson and Rudolf Meidner for interviews. My academic supervisor Lena Sommestad has been a major influence on this book. I also want to extend a thank you to the students who have read the Swedish book as part of their studies and who have been a great source of inspiration in the process of rewriting it in English. Thanks, as always, to all in the Department of Economic History at Uppsala University, as well as to a long row of people in the Institute for Futures Studies and the Institute for Contemporary History in Stockholm, the FOSAM (Forum for contemporary history) in Oslo, the European University Institute in Florence, and the conference network Rethinking Social Democracy. Thanks to all at Manchester University Press, and a final, heartfelt, thank you to my translator Mireille Key, who did a wonderful job at turning my PhD-prose Swedish into more fluent English. In my final rewriting and editing I have mishandled her translation, and I thank her also for forgiving me for this.

I want to dedicate this book to my grandfathers, Hans Olsson and Tage Andersson; one with a certain amount of scepticism for Social Democracy and the institutions of the 'people's home', the other with a blind faith in the party.

Introduction

'Social policy is not a cost – but a productive investment', wrote the Swedish social democratic economist Gunnar Myrdal in 1932, the year the Swedish Social Democratic party (SAP) gained electoral power.[1] This idea of social policy as a productive investment became a core feature in the ideology of Swedish Social Democracy and a central component in the discursive foundation of the Swedish welfare state. The expansion of public responsibility for social security that took place in the post-war period was based on the notion of security and social citizenship as the foundation for an efficient society, and indeed as a prerequisite for future economic growth. However, as the SAP embarked on its 'third way' in the late 1970s and early 1980s, its understanding of social policy as a productive investment seemed to have been replaced by the identification of social policy as a cost and a drain on resources.

The book is about this ideological turnaround and how the notion of the productive role of social policy has changed in the SAP's economic and social policy discourse in the post-war period, from its ideology of the 'strong society' in the 1950s and 1960s, to the attempts to articulate an ideology around the notion of a third way in the early 1980s. The analysis focuses on the two key ideological concepts – 'security' (*trygghet*) and 'growth' (*tillväxt*) – and how they are constructed and articulated in social democratic discourses on social policy over time, as ideological objectives in harmony or in deep conflict. In line with the notion of productive social policies, the idea that security and growth went hand-in-hand was at the heart of the strong society's ideology. However, in the SAP's 1981 Crisis Programme, which followed the 1970s crisis and the two lost elections of 1976 and 1979, growth and security seemed to have become deeply contradictory ideological goals.[2] This book argues that whereas the successful articulation of a positive and harmonious relationship between growth and security as mutually reinforcing goals can be seen as a central element in the hegemonic position of social democratic ideology in the post-war period, this articulation became increasingly problematic for social democracy beginning in the mid-1960s, as both growth and security became increasingly contested concepts and the idea of a causal relationship between them came into question.

This increasing antagonism around social policy and the welfare state is discussed in the book as two periods of critique of social democracy; the late 1960s and its critique of growth, and the early 1980s and its critique of security.

The main ambition of this book is to discuss the party's shifting discourse around the role of social policy in the economy in the post-war period, and thereby elucidate tensions and contradictions with immediate relevance to social policy and social democracy that heretofore have received little attention in studies of the Swedish Labour movement. There is plenty of literature in English about Swedish social democracy and its social and economic theory in the 'golden era'.[3] However, very little (and almost nothing in English) has been written about the party's changing ideology in the crisis-ridden decades of the 1960s, 1970s and 1980s.[4] This book hopes to fill this gap, for instance, by presenting readings of party material from programmes to archival sources that have not yet come to the attention of English-speaking readers. Secondly, it focuses on the relationship between social democracy and critique, and on the complex origins and trajectories of third way discourse between left and right. In passing, the book sheds a critical light on the contemporary, particularly British, discourse within the third way, where social policy is conceptualised precisely as an investment (often with reference to Scandinavian influences), whereas ideas of social citizenship, solidarity and equality seem to differ fundamentally from Swedish universalism.

Notes

1 Myrdal, G., 1932a, 'Socialpolitikens dilemma' I, *Spektrum* 1, pp. 1–13, and Myrdal G., 1932b, 'Socialpolitikens dilemma II', *Spektrum*, 2, pp. 13–31, Stockholm. I have used the abbreviation SAP throughout the book. Today the correct name for the Social Democratic party is *socialdemokraterna.*

2 SAP, 1981a, *Framtid för Sverige* (*A future for Sweden*), Stockholm.

3 See works such as Esping-Andersen, G., 1985, *Politics against markets. The social democratic road to power*, Princeton University Press, Princeton; Tilton, T., 1990, *Through the welfare state to revolution. The political theory of Swedish social democracy*, Clarendon, Oxford; Heclo, H. and Madsen, H., 1987, *Policy and politics in Sweden. Principled pragmatism*, Temple University Press, Philadelphia; Misgeld, K., Molin, K. and Åmark, K. (eds), 1992, *Creating social democracy. A century of the social democratic labour party in Sweden*, Pennsylvania State University Press, Philadelphia.

4 The main works on Swedish third way policies in English are Ryner, M., 2000, *Lessons from the Swedish model*, Routledge, New York; Blyth, M., 2002, *Great transformations: Economic ideas and institutional ideas in the 20th century*, Harvard University Press, Boston; Lindvall, J., 2004, *The politics of purpose. Macroeconomic policymaking in Sweden*, doctoral thesis, Department of Political Science, Gothenburg University, Gothenburg. In Swedish, important works are Lundberg, U., 2003, *Juvelen i kronan*, Hjalmarson-Högberg, Stockholm (see in English Lundberg, U., 2005, 'Social democracy lost. The social democratic party in Sweden and the politics of pension reform 1978–1998', working report, Institute for Future Studies, Stockholm); Stråth, B., 1998, *Mellan två fonder*, Atlas, Stockholm; Mellbourn, A., 1986, *Bortom det starka samhället*, Tiden, Stockholm. In addition,

there are now a number of memoirs, importantly those of the Minister of Finance Kjell-Olof Feldt (Feldt, K.-O., 1991, *Alla dessa dagar, I regeringen 1982–1990,* Norstedts, Stockholm) and those of the party leader and Prime Minister Ingvar Carlsson (Carlsson, I., 2003, *Så tänkte jag. Politik och dramatik,* Hjalmarson och Högberg, Stockholm).

1

Between growth and security

Building the people's home

The institutions of the Swedish welfare state have been understood as being grounded in the economic and social policies that developed in response to the 1930s Depression.[1] The 1930s were a formative era, defined by pervasive feelings of national, economic, social and demographic crisis. The 1930s' political debates in Sweden were coloured by Gunnar and Alva Myrdal's discussions on the population question and of 'a national suicide' following dramatically falling birth rates; by the intense debate on adequate policy responses to the Depression that took place in the Stockholm School and the Unemployment Commission; and by the Labour movement's rallying behind the universal, or 'general', social policies that are associated with the minister of social affairs Gustav Möller.[2] What developed in the 1930s in reaction to the Depression was a kind of socio-economic theory that constituted the conceptual underpinnings of the welfare state and paved the way for policies to come. This theory was construed around a set of key metaphors and discursive elements that linked the economic and the social sphere, defined the role of politics for national progress and put in place a social democratic language around the emerging welfare state.

In the interwar period, the SAP had abandoned the overthrow of capitalism in favour of piecemeal reformism. The emphasis of functional socialism, as the theoretical underpinning of the 1930s debates, was no longer the nationalisation of production, but rather the successful amelioration of the social sphere through the socialisation of consumption, social engineering and welfare reform.[3] The concept of the people's home (*folkhemmet*) was introduced into social democratic ideology in a speech by the party leader Per Albin Hansson in 1928. The people's home, an old metaphor, well established in Swedish political language, drew on a conservative and organic legacy of *folk* (people) and nation.[4] The notion of the people's home, moreover, drew on a specific interpretation of national efficiency, one that stressed the interdependencies between economic and social development. The question of providing welfare for the Swedish people was not just a question of social responsibility or solidarity; welfare was directly linked to progress and national development in the economic sense as well. Thus, the concept of welfare had a strong link to the concept of efficiency. The idea of a people's home as the organising metaphor of social democratic ideology from the 1930s onwards captured the notion that social democracy had a responsibility for the national interest: an interest that was broader and not confined to a specific working class. The concept of the people's home was the SAP's attempt to broaden its ideology from fractionary class politics to articulations that contained an overall responsibility for national unity. It was organic, or holistic, all-encompassing, stressing social peace, economic integration, and national renewal. The concept of 'home' was linked to the notion of *samhälle*, society, a notion that in Swedish is deeply connected to the concept of *folk* and denies both the dichotomy of market and state, and the troika of market, state and civil society, in favour of the idea of a home where state and citizen are intrinsically linked. [5] Through the expanding egalitarian institutions of the state, the individual could be liberated from dependency on 'archaic' and bourgeois institutions such as the family, the market or the patriarchal employer. The Swedish historian Lars Trägårdh argues that

> The People's Home was a *folkstat*; the state was the homely domain of national community, the context in which the ideal of solidarity could be joined to that of equality.[6]

To this extent, the notion of the people's home also carried a strong notion of a common economic and social good, a notion that spilled over into economic discourse and the 'social Keynesianism' of the Stockholm School, which was concerned not only with macro-economic policy but also with the planning and rationalisation of the social sphere.[7]

Gunnar Myrdal wrote his articles on the role of social policy in 1932, the year social democracy came into parliamentary power. In two articles, he coined the phrase 'productive' or 'prophylactic' social policy, for social policies with long-term structural effects on national efficiency. Myrdal did not view his intervention as primarily an ideological one, but rather as a scientific and economic one that set out a 'rational' role for social policy in a modern, planned, economy. Prophylactic social policies were directed at the entire structure of the economy and not at the individual symptoms of social problems. Such a social policy, which would effectively do away with social problems as a matter of structural economic engineering (indeed, the article was published in the functionalist architecture journal *Arkitektur och samhälle*) was, according to Myrdal, accurately understood as an investment, just like any other investment in production factors. Myrdal used this notion of investment to set his modern, rational social policies against the existing poor relief system, which he defined as a *de facto* destruction of social capital whose price to society was the cost and waste of social destruction.[8]

Myrdal's discussion bore the stamp of the economic discourse that surrounded the social question from the mid-nineteenth century onwards. In the German historical school, social policy was identified primarily as a means of economic policy directed at the efficient organisation of society's social resources and at counteracting the destructive effects of uncurbed industrial capitalism on social structures and on the economy as a whole. In this deeply conservative discussion in Imperial Germany, social policy was hardly a matter of individual rights, but rather a form of mercantilist politics directed at the lower strata of society.[9] German *Kathedersocialismus* had a decisive influence on Swedish economic thought at the turn of the century, and particularly on the conservative and liberal economists of the Old Stockholm School. Gustaf Cassel and Eli Heckscher, key figures in the older generation of Stockholm School economists, were both deeply committed to issues of poverty and engaged in the Swedish equivalent of the *Verein fur Sozialpolitik*, the Association for social work (CSA, *Centralförbundet för socialt arbete*). In 1902, Cassel introduced central elements of German social policy discourse into the Swedish debate in his book *Socialpolitiken* (*Social Policy*). Cassel had studied with Adolf Wagner in Germany, and he himself became the young Gunnar Myrdal's tutor.[10]

Until the 1930s, Swedish political culture was heavily influenced by German conservative discourse. Influences were, however, not limited to Germany. At the turn of the twentieth century, similar ideas were put forth by proponents of early socialism and English Fabianism and by progressive American economists such as John Commons and Richard Ely.[11] Certainly, the early discourse of the SAP drew on both German *Katedersocialismus* and English Fabianism, merging into what has been described as a sort of pragmatic socio-economic attitude.[12] The doctrines of rationalisation, as they developed in the thinking of Ernst Wigforss, drew on elements from Austrian Marxism, but Wigforss was also inspired by the British ethical socialist Tawney.[13]

However, similar to the way in which the notion of the people's home fell back on an older conservative legacy, the 1930s ideas of the economic role of social policy also fell back on a legacy of discourses that were concerned with social order, efficiency and national unity. These discourses rejected an orthodox *laissez faire* view of free competition because of moral outrage with the destructive effects of capitalism, but they were only mildly concerned with individual emancipation or social transformation. The 1930s discourse of national crisis, however, meant a radicalisation of the socio-political debate and a polarisation of the political spectrum, in which these ideas were appropriated by Swedish social democracy in its attempts to rearticulate itself as a force for the gradual and long-term transformation of capitalism.

Myrdal saw the significance of his ideas for such an ideologically radicalised reformism. To him, an approach to social policy as a productive investment could provide a discursive defence for a significantly expanded role for social policy. The concept of investment had important ideological currency. At the heart of the Swedish economic debate on the Depression was the question of expansion or retraction as a way out of the crisis. Not only did it split the political spectrum between Social Democrats and Liberals; it also caused a split between the old Stockholm School and its liberal and conservative economists, who argued for restraint and for limits on public spending, and progressive economists like Myrdal in the new Stockholm School, who saw in the Depression a new role for the state. The ideas of the new Stockholm School on the role of public expenditure and demand management for employment and macro-economic stability preceded many of the thoughts that Keynes put forward in the *General Theory*. Myrdal observed that the question of public expenditure, and particularly the question of the cost of new social policies, had become a key point of contestation between Liberals and Social Democrats. To Myrdal, the liberal debate, centered on the idea of cost, was irrational, unscientific and propagandistic. But a social democratic definition of social policy as a productive investment would be a strictly scientific argument in line with modern economic thinking. Myrdal's polemic *Kosta sociala reformer pengar?* (*Do social reforms cost money?*) was a scathing critique of the old Stockholm School and the state of orthodox economic thinking in Sweden and the way it had failed to see the strategic roles of public expenditure and welfare reform for the modernisation of the economy.[14] As the purpose of the social policy was not only to create security but to also influence national revenues, Myrdal argued that it could not be considered a cost. Social policy was not only concerned with redistribution of resources, but with the actual creation of an economic surplus. [15]

The SAP embraced Myrdal's idea of the productive role of social policies, and the concept of 'productive social policies' quickly became a trope in party language. Alva and Gunnar Myrdal's population economics and their socially authoritarian ideas of how to best solve the demographic problem clashed with the party leadership over issues of individual rights. The party traditionally understood population economics as a conservative school of thought that laid the double burden of production and reproduction on the working classes.[16] Nonetheless, Myrdal's argument on the economic role of social policy was quite consistent with a 1930s social democratic world of ideas. It fitted in well with the emphasis on an overarching responsibility for economy and welfare in the people's home concept; with functional socialism's preoccupation with consumption and social amelioration; and with the place of public consumption and demand management in the 'new economic ideas' of the party's main theorist Ernst Wigforss. Myrdal's notion of productive social policies also fitted in well with the ideas of universalism that were formulated in Gustav Möller's discussion on comprehensive or 'general' social policies that would not stigmatise the working class in the way that the poor relief system did, but provide security as a matter of right.[17] In the 1930s debate, elements of these different but interconnected discourses fused and merged into a worldview that linked social and economic affairs into a coherent theory of society. The 'new economic ideas' of the macro sphere spilled over onto the micro sphere and family life also became the object of social intervention, planning and rationalisation in the name of the common good. The 1930s set in place a discursive framing around social policy that remained in the post-war period as a specific, social democratic worldview of the relationship between the creation of economic growth and individual security. The foundation for social democracy's outlook on the role of social policy in the national economy was laid – that which creates security also creates growth.

Growth and security: a discursive tenet of reformism

The emphasis on gradual reformism and the expansion of the welfare state as the central route to capitalist transformation made social policy a core component of Swedish social democratic ideology and of the famous 'model' as it developed in the post-war period. The concept of security (*trygghet*) came to the fore of party ideology within the ideology of the strong society beginning in the mid-1950s. It was deeply connected to notions of a growing public responsibility for individual wellbeing, of the role of collective solidarity in the industrial society and to notions of equality and freedom. Security, in social democratic language, had a broad meaning that went beyond issues of material concern and appealed to notions of comfort, wellbeing and belonging. This notion of security was already implicit in the 1930s idea of a people's home. The people's home was not a house with walls and ceiling of material security, but a home built on values such as respect, solidarity and the recognition of need. In post-war party discourse, with its heavy emphasis on technological advancement, modernisation and rapid economic transformations, the concept of security also became a reference to social democracy's capacity to accommodate individual needs in the process of change and the party's ability to protect the individual from the harmful effects of structural transformations. To this extent, the notion of security became intrinsically linked to social democracy's perception of progress and its post-war ideas of the welfare state as a higher form of social development.

But in party rhetoric, security was also given a direct relationship to efficiency, as a precondition for change and, indeed, for the successful creation of an industrial society. The Swedish mixed economy, with its emphasis on planning and rationalisation, embodied the idea that economic and social advances drew on each other and that a modern economy needed a high degree of planning to create gains in efficiency for social welfare purposes. The continued expansion of the welfare state was a crucial part of such a strategy. The underlying theory of the Swedish model of organised capitalism can be seen as a careful balance between social and economic objectives. Economic policy had social welfare ends. The objectives and means of social policy were formulated in a close interaction with active labour market policies and contributed to what has been described as a supply-side orientation that focused on the labour market's need for labour.[18]

This balance between economic and social objectives took expression in social democratic language, as a discourse in which economic concepts such as efficiency or productivity were vested with social content, while concepts denoting the social sphere were also embedded in a sometimes economistic approach to society. For instance, the concept of efficiency was defined in economic policy in the 1950s as social efficiency (*samhällsekonomisk effektivitet*), meaning efficiency in both the economic and the social sense. In particular, security and growth emerged in party rhetoric as overarching ideological elements that were constantly linked to one another. In this manner, security was articulated as not only compatible with, but necessary for, growth, and as an integral element in the creation of an efficient society. Through socio-political measures, one could intervene in production, protect the individual from the negative effects of market conditions and bring about the efficient allocation of labour resources, thereby increasing the quantity and quality of the workforce; facilitating the participation of individuals in production; and increasing demand and purchasing power through allowances and transfers. Family policy was an investment in future social resources.[19]

Correspondingly, in social democratic ideology, *in*security (*otrygghet*) resulting from competition between unprotected individuals in the market place or from insufficient public responsibility and collective solidarity, was understood as something that led to poor management of human resources, stagnation and a deeply inefficient society. Thus, security was a force for economic advancement. On the other hand, the centrality of the concept of growth in Swedish social democratic ideology, with its well-noted productivism, supply side orientation and 'business friendly' corporatism, stemmed from an articulation of economic growth as a force for social progress and, ultimately, as the fundamental means for security.[20]

In the post-war period then, an articulation that stressed the interdependency between growth and security emerged at the core of social democratic ideology. It drew on the notion of productive social policies but went beyond it, as it defined security and growth as two sides of the same coin and made this articulation a central tenet of social reformism. The Danish sociologist Gösta Esping-Andersen has described this particular conceptualisation of welfare reform as a productive investment as Swedish social democracy's way out of the classic equality–efficiency dilemma. In the ideology of Swedish social democracy, this was not a dilemma nor a trade-off, but rather a mutually reinforcing relationship.[21]

This articulation of growth and security as ends in harmony can be seen as a central element in the hegemonic position of the SAP and of social democratic ideology in the post-war period. The ideological ability to tie together social security and economic efficiency was a vital component of social democratic ideology and its capacity to create a consensus around the welfare state and entrench its values in Swedish political culture. It was a normative and ontological worldview through which social democracy perceived, regarded and made sense of economic and social policy problems and articulated a strategy of reform. It was also a central discursive strategy in defence of the welfare state, a dominant articulation through which social democracy could meet rival articulations from both the left and the right. On the one hand, by articulating growth as a social force, social democracy could defend the value of social reformism and meet rival articulations from the left with references to its capacity to create individual security within the capitalist economy and steer growth in the direction of a more equal, and socially inclusive society. On the other, the expansion of social policy could be defended as an economic investment against liberal conceptualisations of social policy as cost. This is reminiscent of how the third way, in Anglo-Saxon discourse, has emphasised the strategic value in seeing social justice and economic efficiency as two sides of the same coin.[22]

To this extent the SAP's understanding of a reciprocal relationship between growth and security meant a strengthening of its ambitions in social policy. However, this duality between growth and security also reproduced the central tension within social democratic ideology between, on the one hand, the regulation of growth and production for security and welfare purposes and, on the other, the fundamental recognition of the primacy of the economy and social democracy's embracing of industrial capitalism. By definition, welfare capitalism is about embedding capitalism in the institutions of the welfare state, thereby strengthening capitalism.[23] The particular growth orientation of the Swedish welfare state also created a deep duality in Swedish social policies, where means such as rehabilitation, care, social insurances and social services were both the tools for intervention into capitalism and the tools for the strengthening of capitalism. Through this duality, social policy became directly linked to production and, despite the importance of the idea of security in post-war policies, also inherently subordinate to a hegemonic objective of economic growth. To that extent, the productivism of Swedish social policies meant a defence of social policy and an argument for extensive social citizenship, but also a constant limitation on social policy discourse and a conditionality to social rights. [24]

Universalism and productivism: a Swedish notion of social citizenship

Since the publication of Gösta Esping-Andersen's famous discussion of the three worlds of welfare capitalism, the Swedish welfare state has been understood as a social model built on the value of universal social citizenship. To this extent, it has often been seen as the opposite of the liberal model, something that is also a pervasive self-image in Swedish politics. This book applies a more critical perspective. It is concerned with productivism as a discourse that contains both a strengthening of social citizenship and an inherent conditionality; secondly, it focuses on the changing nature of productivism over time as a central part of both the ideological change of the SAP and of the change of the Swedish welfare state.

Esping-Andersen, and other observers of the Swedish welfare state, have argued that the productivism of Swedish social policies was an important motivating factor for the universalism of the Swedish welfare state.[25] A Swedish outlook on social policy as productive and as part of an overall socio-economic strategy meant that social policy was not, as in the liberal model, restricted to the residual role of dealing with the worst effects of capitalism on the social sphere, but was designed as an institutionally redistributive strategy for decommodification and equality. In line with this argument, productivism is not workfare, in the sense of social rights being conditional upon productive participation, but rather it is a stress on the productive potential of individuals.[26] There is a significant difference between the social democratic and the liberal tradition in the emphasis on rights on the one hand, and obligations on the other, and in the emphasis on the structural conditions for social problems on the one hand, and the emphasis on individual motivations or incentives on the other. For instance, the contemporary social investment discourse of New Labour differs substantially from Swedish productivism in that it focuses on individual obligation and responsibility, but does not emphasise the productive effects of the rights-side of social citizenship. Swedish productivism certainly emphasised productive participation; however, it also recognised the need for security and the pivotal role of public responsibility and collective solidarity to bring out that productive potential in people. Reciprocity, in this Swedish interpretation, was not about an exchange between rights and responsibilities, but about the recognition that individuals could find themselves in a time of need and that solidarity was a question of extending help with the knowledge that help would be reciprocated when necessary. The Swedish unwillingness to speak in terms of deserving or undeserving poor or indeed of welfare as a kind of contractual exchange relationship, reflects this idea of reciprocity based on the recognition of need, but also based on the presumption that everyone will participate to capacity in production. It is an idea that was rooted in the historic folk ideology of a society that was poor but, compared to other industrialising nations, very equal; a society marked by the virtual absence of an upper class and everyone's participation in, first, agrarian and eventually industrial, production.[27]

On the other hand, and in contrast to Esping-Andersen's positive interpretation of productivism as a strengthening of universalism, it is clear that the SAP, in line with how social democracy generally has to be seen as a social movement historically construed around ideas of the male wage earner, and perhaps even especially so because if its explicit growth orientation, carried a work ethic. This ethic sometimes gave rise to rather disciplinary perspectives and expressed itself in an idea of universalism that directly linked social citizenship to labour market participation. The party's interpretation of universalism, from the 1930s formulation of rights-based universal social policies in the discourse of the minister of social affairs Gustav Möller, dealt with the groups within production, while the party's ideological interest in groups on the margins of or outside the labour market was both circumscribed and much more conditional. This conditionality is reflected in the fundamental institutional duality in the Swedish welfare state between strong universal social rights in the social insurance system – where income relation provides a direct link to individual labour market participation – and much more conditional, means-tested rights in the benefits system that apply to those outside the labour market. To this extent, productivism is not just a discursive foundation of universalism, but also a source of differentiation between productive and unproductive groups in society. It has been suggested that, in the Swedish context, the discursive prerequisite of universalism was indeed the gate-keeping and exclusion of those who did not contribute to the system but who challenged the solidarity of others. A crucial aspect of the notion of the people's home was that it was a democratic vision. From the 1930s, Swedish politics took a decisive stand for democratic development and thus parted ways with a German discourse around social policies and a fascist interpretation of *volk*.[28] Whereas in Nazi Germany, ideas of national efficiency led to the legitimisation of totalitarian social policies in the name of the common good, the Swedish notion of productive social polices contained a strong emphasis on individual rights. This emphasis on rights was, however, not universal in the sense that it applied to everyone. Clearly, the involuntary sterilisations of the mentally handicapped and 'asocial' in Swedish society, which lasted from the 1930s to the 1970s, were also an expression of an idea of efficiency that, when applied to these categories, was allowed to breach individual rights.[29] In defence of his productive social policy reforms, the legendary minister of social affairs Gustav Möller wrote that they were by no means intended for 'asocial elements'. They were intended for 'productive workers' and they should not be misunderstood as if they were about handouts to society's outcasts. Möller's argument here was an almost direct repetition of the one used by the conservative economist Cassel who, in his call for an expanded social policy at the turn of the century, also defined social policy as an economic policy that was about creating national economic efficiency by strengthening productive workers. Social policy was not a 'hothouse for weak plants'.[30] Thus, the heart of Swedish universalism embodied a fundamental distinction between productive workers and asocial elements, between those to whom universalism applied, based on their productive input, and those to whom it did not apply, based on the nature of their asocial behaviour, and the threat that this posed to the solidarity necessary for universalism. Social rights were essentially linked to production.

This link between social rights and the needs of production served not only as a kind of template in the 1930s for how social democracy thought about social groups and social needs. Perceptions about social problems and needs have been posited against understandings of the needs of production, and productivist notions of the requirements of economic growth have tainted and even defined social democracy's perception of socially problematic groups within social policy and given rise to categories and definitions of social problems. Moreover, productivism is a historical and changing notion, whose place and meaning in social democratic ideology has changed over time, in line with changes in interpretations of the surrounding economic and social world and with different social democratic conceptualisations of what societal activities constitute added value. Whereas the productivity argument of the 1930s social policy and the strong society constituted the motivating factors for socio-political expansion and heightened expectations vis-à-vis socially problematic groups, in later periods, conceptions regarding the need to create growth and economic effectiveness led instead to a calling into question of the economic role of social policy. I argue that this development coincides with and is mirrored in a development wherein social democracy's conceptualisations of the groups within social policy and on the margins of the labour market as a productive labour reserve have been replaced with the construction of a social group of weak, disabled and socially excluded individuals, who are seen as a cost to, and a drain on, society's solidarity. This change is arguably one of the core elements of Swedish third way policies, and it says a lot about the ideological changes in contemporary social democracy.

Between left and right: the SAP from a strong society to a third way

In the, by now, vast body of international literature on the third way, the rise of third way policies have been interpreted as a process of disembeddedness that, contrary to the way in which welfare capitalism gradually embedded the market economy in social institutions, gradually deregulated and did away with those arrangements. Third way thinking has introduced a turnaround in the power hierarchy between economic and social objectives. The place of the economy in social democratic ideology has shifted decisively, from a sphere of intervention in the name of the social good, to a sphere largely outside of the realm of politics and ideology, one that is governed by the logic of forces that are understood as outside of political control. This naturalisation of the economy has resulted in new discourses around social reform – discourses that have centred in on the needs of the market economy.[31]

Clearly, the third way is a heterogeneous and divergent project that takes many different forms in different national political cultures, but there are also important commonalities.[32] On a general level, the third way has meant a reappraisal of market arrangements, which has resulted in a process of rearticulation of 'classical' social democratic objectives, such as equality and security in relationship to understandings of what the market economy requires. An often quoted example is New Labour's reinterpretation of 'equality' to 'equality of opportunity' in adaptation to the demands of post-fordist labour markets. In British welfare reform, the concept of security has become intrinsically linked to the market through the introduction of new reforms, such as public–private partnerships or private finance initiatives that promote market and competitive conditions.[33] The process of market appraisal has, to a large extent, concerned a re-evaluation of means, particularly around the balance between the public and the private in welfare reform. However, these new means reflect changing values regarding which activities are deemed productive as well as a definite tilt in favour of private solutions at times. Means such as new public management, which are modelled on neoclassical understandings of the public sector's *modus operandi*, clearly reflect a market template for understandings of efficiency. In a sense, the rise of third way policies parallels the 'new deal' policies of the 1930s. They draw on new intellectual foundations, such as monetarism and the social philosophy of neo-liberalism, which have led to new conceptualisations of the interplay between economic and social progress. Similar to the way in which the Keynesian new economic ideas of the 1930s surrounding the macro level translated from the macro level's framings to framings around individual social problems, monetarism has translated to understandings of problems such as unemployment or social exclusion as rooted in individual dispositions and 'employability', and as something that must, to a certain extent, be accepted for the efficient working of the economy.[34] The third way also frames social problems in the language of economic efficiency. This economic language, however, is a different language from the one that shaped the welfare state.

Much of the international literature surrounding the ideological change of contemporary social democracy has tended to see Sweden as a kind of resilient, inherently welfare statist society, built on corporatism, social consensus and a persistent *folkhem* ideology.[35] Swedish social democracy has not developed a third way discourse to the same extreme as Britain has. Instead, it has held on to values such as universalism, full employment and equality. Whereas this is true in the relative sense, that is, in comparison with the more radical changes in social democratic ideology that have taken place elsewhere, it is not true that Swedish social democracy has not changed nor that Swedish welfare policies have not changed in the last decades. In part, this interpretation of Sweden as a resilient people's home is due to the paucity of literature in English and the fact that few observers read Swedish sources. The ambiguous character of Swedish politics in the 1990s and 2000s probably also plays a role. The 1980s saw major changes in the economic and social policy discourse of the SAP – discursive changes that paved the way for the sometimes far-reaching changes in Swedish welfare policies in the 1990s. In the 1980s and 1990s, the door was opened for the privatisation of childcare, elderly care and hospitals; vouchers were introduced in schooling; and the 1994 pension reform stands out as radical in a European perspective in that it links future pensions directly to macroeconomic performance and demographic developments.[36] Many of these policies were deeply unpopular in Swedish society, and the party lost some of its image as the custodian of the people's home. In the late 1990s and early 2000s, the SAP tried to reconnect to its historical articulations and break with the legacy of its third way experiment. Once again, party rhetoric contains echoes of post-war discourses. In particular, there has been a newfound emphasis on the interdependency of growth and security. The new party programme of 2001 states that welfare policy is productive.[37] In a speech to the policy network conference in Budapest in 2004, Prime Minister Göran Persson stated that security is the prerequisite of successful economic change.[38] In the 2005/6 campaign leading up to the 2006 elections, the concept of the people's home once again stood against a social democratic depiction of the American workfare model, where people live in constant insecurity.[39]

The function and meaning of this contemporary party discourse is the subject of another book.[40] Suffice it to say that I am optimistic that these rhetorical moves constitute a party reappraisal of the historical lessons of the Swedish model and an attempt to lay them at the basis of a Swedish strategy for coping with globalisation and structural change. However, as a result of this return to post-war social democratic language, observers of Sweden in the late 1990s and early 2000s describe Swedish politics as a deeply ambiguous project that oscillates between retrenchment policies, on the one hand, and the continuation of a political language of universalism, full employment and security, on the other. This oscillation is also noticeable in party rhetoric and ideology. At pains as it is to establish continuity with the ideology of the strong society and block out the articulations of the third way, the party still has to grapple with the discourses set in place in the 1980s and 1990s and the changing meaning of concepts such as security that these brought about. Moreover, the policies that were introduced in the 1980s and 1990s drew on values that seemed to break with the post-war model, and the policies are, in most cases, still there. For this reason, it is very difficult to understand the nature of contemporary Swedish social democratic politics without putting them in the context of the ideological changes of the 1980s. This process of rearticulation, like those in other periods of modernisation in party history, has left a discursive legacy that also structures the party's attempts to make sense of the world today.

In this book, I attempt to offer what I think is a much-needed rethinking of the Swedish case through what might be described as a history of the Swedish third way and its sometimes rather contradictory origins. The focus of this book is on a historical process characterised by the escalating uncertainty of the social and economic environment and a growing struggle around how to best understand the dual processes of creating security and growth.

Beginning with the late 1960s, the SAP's relationship to the welfare state went from a fairly straightforward one dealing with the addition of one reform to another, to a deeply troublesome one. In the turbulent decades of the 1960s, 1970s and 1980s, the welfare state developed from a proud achievement to something that was the source of both ideological and financial problems and sometimes seemed to weigh the party down.[41] In this process, the SAP's idea of a relationship between growth and security became increasingly problematic. From the late 1960s, in Sweden as in many other places, the general optimism around an industrial society and the promises of industrial growth came to a halt as new problems of social development came to the fore.[42] In Sweden, this period was also characterised by a rejuvenated debate on inequality and by the advent of new social movements for international solidarity, gender equality and other concerns, such as a clean environment – demands that were far from the content of social democratic ideology in the previous decades. To the SAP, these ideological changes put a dramatic end to its hegemonic position in the relative consensus around the welfare state in the 1950s and early 1960s. From the late 1960s onwards, the key concepts in social democratic ideology – growth, equality, solidarity and security – were all contested. Particularly awkward for the SAP was the fact that a new generation of the Swedish left singled out its productivist orientation, dismissing it as a far too complacent attitude towards capitalism. The question of the relationship between growth and social progress became a hotspot, something that also called for its rethinking and rearticulation in social democratic ideology. Much of the SAP's ideological changes in the following decades were attempts to meet this critique and incorporate its demands into social democratic ideology.

In the period beginning with the mid-1970s, the question of growth became even more pressing, not because of its ideological centrality but because of its rapid erosion. The post-war period's optimistic ideas of growth as a constant in the process of change were replaced with a deep concern about how to recreate growth as the material foundation of the Swedish welfare state. This triggered another process of rearticulation of social democratic ideology, where its post-war articulations around affluence were replaced by the ideological adaptation to the society of permanent austerity.[43] In this process, growth gained a decisive ideological upper hand and party policy focused on handling the economic crisis, despite the continued expansion of the welfare state in certain key areas, such as childcare, until the mid-1970s. From the late 1970s, an increasingly radicalised Swedish right, influenced by Thatcherism and Friedmanomics, targeted the welfare state and the public sector as the central problem of the Swedish economy and began mobilising for an end to social democratic power.[44] Against the social democratic notion of security it put the concept of freedom. As the SAP regained a majority in the *Riksdag* after having lost two elections in 1976 and 1979, the party seemed to have taken over and internalised many of these framings.[45] The Crisis Programme in 1981 launched the idea of a third way. In this early 1980s interpretation, the third way meant that it was neither Mitterand-style Keynesianism, nor Thatcherism, but a Swedish middle way between retractionary policies and saving on the one hand, and saving jobs and welfare arrangements on the other.[46] Fifteen years before the international centre-left project of the third way, the Swedish third way included many elements of what has since become third way discourse in the UK and elsewhere: namely, decentralisation, freedom of choice and the marketisation of welfare. It also opened the way for a fundamental re-evaluation of core postulates of the post-war model and the ideology of the welfare state. The idea that the expansion of security could be linked to economic expansion in a growing public sector was dismissed as an outdated ideology, one that was out of step with a dramatically altered economic reality. The SAP even shunned the notion of the people's home, depicted by the Swedish right as a quasi-totalitarian, cradle-to-grave system that suffocated individual freedom.

Revisionism and ideological articulation: means and ends

In the following pages, I suggest that this process can be understood as a growing tension between the concepts of security and growth in social democratic ideology, gradually leading up to a turnaround in the hierarchy between the two concepts and their standing as means and ends in relation to one another.

The question of means and ends is key to the discussion of the third way. Social Democrats have claimed that the third way represents the pragmatic reconsideration of means in order to uphold the classical, eternal values of social democracy.[47] This argument is almost essential to the process of ideological revisionism; it was used by social democratic modernisers in the 1950s and 1960s, it has been used extensively by New Labour to legitimise its modernisation strategy, and indeed it was at the core of the Swedish third way.[48] Often, this question of means goes well beyond a technical discussion of the means of reform to fundamental debates on the meaning of overarching ideological concepts, such as efficiency, equality and security. The process of revisionism is concerned with the rearticulation of central ideological elements, with explaining why they are compatible or why they are not, and what must take priority in order to bring about a better society in the long-term perspective. Consequently, this process is concerned with how overarching objectives such as growth and security, equality and efficiency relate to one another as the means to ends, and with the power hierarchy of such concepts.

This process of articulating and rearticulating such relationships is not a question of mere pragmatism, but the rearticulation of the means to ends, and changes in the hierarchy of overarching ideological concepts is indeed a core feature of the process of ideological change, one that eventually leads to what must be described as a new ideology. Ideology is a worldview, a framing that actively creates meaning and significance for a complex reality and defines how social and economic processes should be understood and described, thereby creating coherence and consistent interpretations of complex causal relationships. Economy and production are also a part of a social ontology, a reality that first derives meaning through the discursive and ideological creation of meaning. In this sense, the ideological articulation, 'growth creates security', embodies a completely different worldview than does 'growth creates insecurity' and, to put it bluntly, 'security creates growth' is not the same ideology as 'security does not create growth'. The articulation of the meaning of and relationship between such overarching ideological objectives is a central part of the political struggle. In other words, the ideological struggle is about the meaning sphere, the substance of political concepts and the manner in which the relationship between them should be understood. Thus, the way in which such overarching ideological concepts are articulated and their relationship to each other is not a fight over rhetoric, but a struggle over the power of how to define the world, in competition with other worldviews and alternative images of reality. This rearticulation of the means to ends is a central aspect of the process of revisionism and, by definition, involves the standing of key ideological elements and their interrelationship. When this changes, so does ideology.[49]

Growth and security are master concepts in social democratic ideology, concepts that in the political struggle, however, are deeply controversial to the point of being essentially contested. They embody ideological goal formulations and visions – ideas of what is socially and economically desirable, as well as notions as to what is required to achieve these goals and create growth and security. The notion of security specifies a level of ambition within social policy and sets a horizon for the process of social problem solving; it also defines the relationship between the individual and politics in this process. Other conceptual expressions regarding what is required to create security – for whom and by what means – are articulated in relationship to it. In Swedish discourse, the security concept includes formulations on the relationship of growth to security, as well as on the roles that security and social policy play for growth and notions of the role of public and private in this process. Growth is a powerful definition of progress and a specific outlook on what constitutes productive and value-adding activities.[50] Growth has always been a central preoccupation of social democracy, usually articulated as a means to other desirable ends, such as the eradication of poverty and inequality. In short, growth is something of a constant in social democratic ideology. However, the meaning of the concept of growth and its standing in relation to other means or ends is not fixed; rather it is constantly changing in social democratic discourse, to the extent that at times it has been an instrumental value for other ideological priorities, whereas at other times it has been close to becoming an ideological priority in and of itself. Another crucial question for social democratic history is how social democracy has thought about the process of wealth creation, that is, what creates growth, and the role of the welfare state in that process.[51] One can say that growth and security have existed in a shifting means–end relationship, with changing understandings of their causal connections over the periods. The relationship between these two concepts in social democratic ideology can be said to constitute a discourse around social policy, social reality, social needs and the nature of the social policy problem, which co-exists with other framings in the struggle over the power to define reality.

From this perspective, the book's main argument is that Swedish third way policies can be interpreted as a major ideological turnaround, in which growth took priority over security and security lost its role for growth. This, however, was a complex process, and it is important not to fall into the trap that views the third way as a radical break with all that social democracy ever stood for. Revisionism and ideological modernisation are essentially processes of reinterpreting the ideological framework through new articulations of key elements and their interdependence, but this rarely happens as a clean break. Rather, the very process of ideological revisionism is deeply concerned with the reinterpretation of the ideological legacy, and shifts of meaning do not take place in the form of radical reinvention but in the form of rereading existing meanings and through new layers that are added to them. Similar to the way in which British New Labour went back to reading Crosland to find ideological legitimacy for new conceptualisations of the third way in the mid-1990s, the SAP went back to the writings of Tage Erlander and Ernst Wigforss to find legitimacy for its third way in the early 1980s.

Critique and reaction

This book is concerned with Swedish social democracy's relationship in the post-war period, with growing critique from both left and right and with the gradual process from social democratic reaction to rearticulation and ideological change. In particular, it focuses on the way in which discourses, concepts and metaphors used *in the critique of* social democratic ideology become integrated elements *in* social democratic ideology and structure processes of ideological rearticulation.

It discusses social democracy's relationship to two periods of radicalisation and the critique that, with roots in Marxism, critical sociology and radical social work, attacked the SAP from the left in the late 1960s, and the critique that, influenced by the rise of neo-liberal thought and monetarist economic ideas, attacked social democracy from the right in the period from the late 1970s to the mid-1980s. Both these periods of critique targeted the welfare state, its ideological underpinnings and its standing in social democratic ideology, and they both rejected social democracy's articulation of a positive relationship between growth and security, albeit from very different perspectives. The 1960s critique and its discussions of social problems associated with industrial growth took the form of a social critique of the concept of growth, whereas the 1980s discourse surrounding the problems of the public sector took the form of an economic critique of the concept of security. Ultimately, the book puts forward the argument that there are important discursive continuities and gradual shifts of meaning between '1968' and the neo-liberal turn of the 1980s and that the Swedish third way draws on continuities that combine elements from both of these discourses.[52]

These radicalisation periods of the late 1960s and early 1980s have been interpreted very differently in Swedish political history. The 1970s have been understood as leading to a short-lived social democratic offensive primarily in industrial policy and economic democracy, an offensive that also opened the door for the 'fall' of the Swedish model because it stepped away from the corporatism of the post-war period and threatened the foundations of the historical compromise between labour and capital.[53] In more recent writings this interpretation has sometimes gone so far as to suggest that the debate on wage earner funds is to blame for the fall of the Swedish model. The 1980s, in turn, have been seen as a thorough-going crisis of social democracy and of the Swedish welfare state in the face of the radicalisation of the Swedish right that caused the final breakdown of corporatism and shifted Swedish political discourse decisively to the right. In the mid-1990s a very influential Swedish study, which that drew on the work of Stuart Hall and others on the rise of Thatcherism in Britain, argued that the mobilisation of the Swedish right had caused a great 'right-wing tide' that by the mid-1980s had washed over all areas of Swedish public debate. By the end of the 1980s, all alternatives to the market economy had left the sphere of public debate and neo-liberalism was truly hegemonic.[54] It is clear that the important shift to the right in Swedish political discourse that occurred in the1980s was related to the international rise of neo-liberalism; it is also clear that this shift to the right penetrated into social democratic ideology. However, the problem with these interpretations of hegemonic neo-liberalism is that they create an image of a powerful tide that sweeps in and drowns other expressions, alternative images and opposing discourses. Social democracy is left as a passive recipient of aggressive neo-liberalism. Its reception, reaction and processes of rethinking end up in the background.[55] More recently, studies have shown that Swedish social democracy lost historical articulations surrounding economic democracy and wage earner funds, labour market policy and pensions to a neo-liberal language that was advocated by a circle of modernisers within the SAP, primarily within what was in Swedish known as the '*kanslihushöger*', the group of economists who under the Minister of Finance Kjell-Olof Feldt took over the Ministry of Finance after the return to parliamentary power in 1982.[56]

Moreover, it is hard to comprehend the complexities and ambiguities of the third way, in Sweden and elsewhere, from a view of the third way as a sudden concession to hegemonic neo-liberalism. The shifts to the right in the 1980s were preceded by shifts to the left in the late 1960s and 1970s, and neo-liberal language took over many of the elements of the new left discourse, for instance, its emphasis on individualism and its hatred of bureaucracy.[57] This continuity is also represented in the way in which the radicalisation of the SAP's economic policies in the 1970s, with investment politics, wage earner funds and economic democracy, opened the door not only to the clash with the Swedish right, but also to a recognition within social democratic ideology of the problems of industry, which in turn led to a *de facto* appraisal of the market in the decades to come. Somehow there was a fine line between the attempts to increase political control over investment in the 1970s and the third way's attempts to transfer resources from the public to the private sector in the 1980s even if the value base was radically different. What in the 1970s was intended as a step further on the road to socialism ended up as a recognition of market capitalism.[58] The element of historic contradiction in this process is important because it keeps us from seeing the third way as a gradual evolution towards a better understanding of economy and market; further, it points to the way that discourses and policy solutions developed in response to a specific problem can take on very different meanings when the problem, in the focus of politics and the surrounding ideological tide, changes.

What then is the relationship between these periods of critique and what is social democracy's position half way between the winds of the left and the great right-wing tide?

This book attempts to provide a historical narrative of the dynamic relationship between the concepts of 'security' and 'growth' in the post-war ideology of the SAP as a dynamic and changing relationship over time, one that is embedded in gradual shifts of meaning in the post-war period. If the hegemony of social democratic ideology and the SAP in the period from the 1930s lay in its ability to represent 'growth' and 'security' as coherent ideological values and the means to the same end, then the post-war period can be understood as an increasingly discursive struggle over this relationship, over the meaning of each concept and over the way the relationship between them should be understood: as mutually supportive and harmonious or as deeply antagonistic. I suggest that, in the Swedish context, the much-discussed 'crisis' of social democracy can be understood as historic moments when this relationship came under question, in processes of antagonism and struggle, which eventually led to rearticulation and ideological change. The aim of this book, therefore, is to problematise our understanding of the change of contemporary social democracy and of the complex and often contradictory origins of third way policies, by focusing on the actors and carriers of discourse, and in particular, on the relationship between radical critique and social democratic reaction and rearticulation.

The critiques of the late 1960s and the early 1980s are both discussed as being *radical*, in the sense that they pointed to perceived discrepancies between social democratic ideology and a dramatically transformed social or economic reality that in some way required a fundamental rethinking of ideological postulates in order to create a better fit between ideology and reality. Thus, I have not associated the term 'radical' with the left, but rather with something that challenges social democratic orthodoxy. However, I also suggest that, in the Swedish case, even radical critique was inherently *reformist*, in the sense that important parts of both of these processes of radicalisation took place in close proximity to the Labour movement itself, in the party, the trade union federation or in the welfare state bureaucracy. In the Swedish context, '1968' did not, for the most part, take revolutionary expression. Much of the political radicalisation of the late 1960s took place around new political cultures, for instance the anti-Vietnam war FNL-movement or the women's rights group, Group 8, which was influential in raising the issue of gender equality and setting women's work and the right to day care on the agenda, but an important part of the late 1960s was that groups in the administration and planning at the heart of the Swedish welfare state turned against policy and against social democracy for not being sufficiently social democratic. This peculiarity has caused observers of Sweden's 1968 to label it 'critical social democracy' rather than revolutionary Marxism.[59] Similarly, the process of neo-liberal radicalisation in the 1980s was not only a matter of the mobilisation of the right, but more importantly of groups within the SAP as well.[60] This may also indicate a tendency of the SAP to incorporate rival articulations into party ideology rather than marginalising them, thereby also silencing them. There is an important difference in political culture here between Swedish labourism and the much more resilient legacy of the new left in, for instance, Britain.

This book, then, also makes a case for understanding social democratic ideological change through the relationship between party ideology and groups that, at different points in time, carry critique and confront party ideology with new images of reality. I believe that this perspective makes it possible to problematise both the late 1960s and the 1980s as periods of critique. It also sheds light on how ideological change occurs and how social democracy handled a changing economic and social reality, in which ideological premises were reformulated following altered requirements and critique, but in which the ideological legacy also created those framings in which social, economic and political changes were managed. The actors discussed in the following chapters – social workers in the 1960s and economists in the 1980s – constitute groups that exist in the border between social democratic ideology and knowledge production in the administration of the welfare state. In their capacity as knowledge groups or brokers of ideas, they provide the descriptions of reality that become the basis for social reform. This is not a peaceful process, but as the political scientist Peter Hall has asserted, policy change often takes place through a struggle over 'authoritative knowledge', a struggle over those images of reality that most convincingly define the surrounding world and that become accepted as accurate representations of the world.[61] Knowledge groups influence the way in which the political problem is defined and posed through definitions of 'what is wrong and what needs to be fixed', thereby setting the course for the problem-solving process.[62] They mediate reality and produce the 'namings' and 'framings' of policy problems necessary for political action; they also advocate selective and constraining representations of reality and of the policy problem. They exist between what may be called the ontological and the ideological – in the sphere between a description of what is and a prescription of what should be done, and in this position, they are powerful critics of social democracy.[63]

Notes

1 See Rothstein, B., 1996, *The social democratic state. The Swedish social model and the bureaucratic problem of social reforms*, University of Pittsburg Press, Pittsburgh.

2 Trägårdh, L., 2002a, 'Crisis and the Politics of National Community', in Witoszek, N. and Trägårdh, L. (eds), *Culture and crisis. The case of Germany and Sweden*, Berghahn Books, New York; Carlson, A., 1990, *The Swedish experiment in family politics. The Myrdals and the interwar population crisis*, Transaction, New Brunswick; Esping-Andersen 1985; Carlsson, B. and Wadensjö, E., 'The committee on unemployment and the Stockholm School', in Jonung, L. (ed.), 1991, *The Stockholm School of economics revisited*, Cambridge University Press, Cambridge; Sommestad, L., 1998, 'Human reproduction and the rise of welfare states. An economic-demographic approach to welfare state formation in the United States and Sweden', *Scandinavian economic history review*, 46.2, pp. 97–116; Esping-Andersen, G. and Korpi, W., 1987, 'From poor relief to institutional welfare states. The development of Scandinavian social policy', *International journal of sociology*, 16, pp. 3–4.

3 Adler-Karlsson, G., 1970, *Funktionssocialism, ett alternativ till kommunism och kapitalism*, Verdandi, Uppsala; Tilton 1991; Esping-Andersen 1985.

4 Lagergren, F., 1999, *På andra sidan välfärdsstaten*, Symposion, Stockholm; Trägårdh, L., 2002b, 'Sweden and the EU. Welfare state nationalism and the spectre of Europe', in Hansen, L. and Waever, O. (eds), *European integration and national identity. The challenge of the Nordic states*, Routledge, London, pp. 130–181.

5 Trägårdh, 2002b; Sejersted, F., 2005, *Socialdemokratins tidsålder: Sverige och Norge under 1900–talet*, Nya Doxa, Nora.

6 Trägårdh 2002b.

7 Skocpol, T. and Weir, M., 1985, 'State structures and the possibilities of Keynesian responses to the Great Depression in the United States, Britain and Sweden', in Skocpol, T., Rueschemeyer, D. and Evans, P., 1985, *Bringing the state back in*, Cambridge University Press, Cambridge, pp. 107–161; Olsson, U., 1994, 'Planning in

the Swedish welfare state', in Clemence, W. and Mahon, R. (eds), *Swedish social democracy. A model in transition*, Canada Studies in Political Economy, Toronto.

8 Myrdal, G., 1932c, 'Kosta sociala reformer pengar?', *Arkitektur och samhälle*, 33 pp. 33–44, Stockholm.

9 Steinmetz, G., 1993, *Regulating the social. The welfare state and local politics in Imperial Germany*, Princeton University Press, Princeton; Andersson, J., 2005, 'A productive social citizenship? The metaphor of productive social policies in the European tradition', in Stråth, B. and Magnusson L. (eds), A *European social citizenship? Future preconditions in historical light*, PIE Peter Lang, Brussels, pp. 69–89; Friman, E., 2002, *No limits. The 20th century discourse of economic growth*, Department of History, Umeå University, p. 84f.

10 Cassel, G., 1902, *Socialpolitiken*, Gebers, Stockholm; Carlsson, B., 1994, *The state as a monster. Gustav Cassel and Eli Heckscher on the role and growth of the state*, University Press of America, Boston; Rodgers, D., 1998, *Atlantic crossings. Social politics in a progressive age*, Harvard University Press, Cambridge, MA; Friman 2002 p. 78f.

11 See Moss, D., 1996, *Socializing security*, Harvard University Press, Cambridge, MA, on the writings of the American progressive economists John Commons and Richard Ely; Beilharz, P. and Nyland, C., 1998 (eds), *The Webbs, Fabianism and Feminism*, Ashgate, Aldershot.

12 Karlsson, S., 2001, *Det intelligenta samhället. En omtolkning av socialdemokratins idéhistoria*, Carlssons, Stockholm.

13 Tilton 1990 p. 51.

14 Myrdal 1932c; Carlsson, B., 1991, 'The long retreat. Gustav Cassel and Eli Heckscher on the New Economics of the 1930s', in Jonung, L. (ed.), *The Stockholm School of economics revisited*, Cambridge University Press, Cambridge.

15 Myrdal 1932c p. 44.

16 Wennemo, I., 1992, 'Arbetarrörelsen och befolkningsfrågan. Knut Wicksell och makarna Myrdals befolkningsteorier', *Arkiv* 50, Stockholm; Rothstein, B., 1998, *Just institutions matter*, Cambridge University Press, Cambridge.

17 Tilton 1990 p. 103 f.; Rothstein, B., 1985, 'Managing the welfare state, lessons from Gustav Möller', *Scandinavian Political Studies*, 8, 3, pp. 151–170; Rothstein 1998 p. 171f.

18 Stephens, J.D., 1979, *The transition from capitalism to socialism*, New Studies in Sociology, London; Ryner 2002.

19 Esping-Andersen 1985 pp. 1–22; Esping-Andersen, G., 1990, *The three worlds of welfare capitalism*, Polity Press, Cambridge, p. 65f.

20 Compare Hinnfors, J., 2005, 'Market-friendly social democracy', paper to the second conference Rethinking Social Democracy, Swansea, April 2005.

21 Esping-Andersen 1985.

22 See Driver, S. and Martell, L., 1998, *New Labour: Politics after Thatcherism*, Polity Press, Cambridge.

23 See Polanyi, K., 2001, *The great transformation, the political and economic origins of our time*, Beacon Press, Boston; Offe, K., 1984, *Contradictions of the welfare state*, Studies in Contemporary German Thought, MIT press, Cambridge, MA.

24 Compare Kulawik, T., 1993, 'A productivist welfare state. The Swedish model revisited', in Borkowski, T. (ed), *Social policies in a time of transformation*, Goethe Institute and Jagellonian University, Krakow; and Kulawik, T., 2002, keynote lecture 'The Nordic model of the welfare state and the trouble with a critical perspective', at

the conference *Norden at the crossroads*, Helsinki, 30 October–2 November 2002.

25 Esping-Andersen 1985, 1990; Tilton 1990.

26 Tilton 1990 p. 164.

27 Sommestad 1998.

28 Berman, S., 1998, *The social democratic moment*, Harvard University Press, Cambridge, MA; Trägårdh 2002b.

29 A new generation of Swedish historians have brought out the darker side of the people's home in terms of eugenics and social discipline. Very little of this has reached beyond the Swedish debate. See Bo Rothstein's debate with Yvonne Hirdman: Hirdman, Y., 2000, *Att lägga livet till rätta, studier i svensk folkhemspolitik*, Carlsson, Stockholm; Rothstein 1998. See also Broberg, G. and Tydén, M., 1996, 'Eugenics in Sweden, efficient care', in Broberg, G. and Roll-Hansen, N. (eds), *Eugenics and the welfare state*, Michigan State University Press, Michigan; Runcis, M., 1998, *Steriliseringar i folkhemmet*, Ordfront, Stockholm; Björkman, J., 2001, *Vård för samhällets bästa*, Carlssons, Stockholm; Spektorowski, A. and Mizrachi, E., 2004, 'Eugenics and the welfare state in Sweden. The politics of social margins and the idea of a productive society', *Journal of contemporary history*, 39, 3, pp. 333–352.

30 Cassel 1902 p. 19.

31 Hall, S., 1998, *Thatcherism and the crisis of the left*, Verso, London; Jessop, B., 2001, *The future of the welfare state*, Polity, Oxford; Driver-Martell 1998; Hay, C., 1999, *The political economy of New Labour. Labouring under false pretences?* Manchester University Press, Manchester; Moschonas, G., 2002, *In the name of social democracy. The great transformation 1945 to the present*, Verso, London.

32 Moschonas 2002; Callaghan, J., 2000, *The retreat of social democracy*, Manchester University Press, Manchester; Giddens, A. (ed.), 2001, *The global third way debate*, Polity Press, Cambridge.

33 Fairclough, N., 2000, *New Labour, new language*, Routledge, London; Powell, M. (ed.), 1999, *New Labour, new welfare state? The third way in British social policy*, Polity Press, London.

34 Byrne, D., 1999, *Social exclusion*, Open University Press, London; Levitas, R., 2005, *The inclusive society. Social exclusion and New Labour*, Palgrave, London; Mann, K., 1999, 'Critical reflections on the underclass and poverty', in Gough, I. and Olofsson, G. (eds), *Capitalism and social cohesion. Essays on exclusion and integration*, Macmillan, London.

35 Merkel, W., 2001, 'The third ways of social democracy', in Giddens 2001 pp. 51–73; Schmidt, V.A. 2000, 'Values and discourse in the politics of adjustment', in Scharpf, F. and Schmidt, V.A. (eds), *Work and welfare in the open economy*, Oxford University Press, Oxford.

36 Palme, J. (ed.), 2002, *Welfare in Sweden. The balance sheet for the 1990s*, Ds 2002:32, Stockholm; Palme, J. and Kangas, O. (eds), 2005, *Social policy and economic development in the Nordic countries*, Palgrave Macmillan, Basingstoke; Palme, J. and Wennemo, I., 1998, *Swedish social security in the 1990s. Reform and retrenchment*, Ministry of Social Affairs, Stockholm; Blomqvist, P., 2004, *Ideas and policy convergence. Health care reforms in the Netherlands and Sweden in the 1990s*, doctoral dissertation, Columbia University; Blomqvist, P. and Rothstein, B., 2000, *Välfärdsstatens nya ansikte*, Agora, Stockholm, Bergqvist, C.; and Nyberg, A., 2002, 'Welfare state reconstruction and child care in Sweden', in Michel, S. (ed.), *Childcare at the crossroads*, Routledge, New York, pp. 287–307.

37 Socialdemokraterna, *Partiprogram 2001*.

38 Persson to the policy network, Budapest 2004: www.policy-network.net.
39 Göran Persson in televised party leader debate, SVT, September 4, 2005.
40 See Andersson, J., 'The people's library and the electronic workshop', paper to the second conference Rethinking Social Democracy, Swansea, April 2005.
41 Lundberg, U. and Petersen, K., 1998, 'Valfaerdsstatens fuldbyrdelse, krise og genkomst: socialdemokratiet i Danmark og Sverige fra 1960erne og frem', *Den jytske historiker*, 82, pp. 92–114.
42 Sasson, D., 1996, *One hundred years of socialism. The west European left in the twentieth century*, IB Tauris, London.
43 Pierson, P. (ed.), 2001, *The new politics of the welfare state*, Oxford University Press, Oxford.
44 Mishra, R., 1984, *The welfare state in crisis. Social thought and social change*, St Martins Press, New York; Ryner 2000.
45 Stråth 1998.
46 Ryner 2000 p. 125f.; Lindvall 2004.
47 See the Labour Party, 1997, *Because Britain deserves better*, London; Blair, T., 1998, *The third way – new politics for the new century*, Fabian Society, London.
48 Moschonas 2002. Compare Favretto, I., 2003, *The long search for a third way*, Palgrave Macmillan, London; Sassoon 1996.
49 Hall, S., 1988, p. 9, and Hall, S., 1996, 'The problem of ideology. Marxism without guarantees', in Hall, S., Morley, D. and Chen, K. (eds), *Critical dialogues in cultural studies*, Routledge, New York/London; Laclau, E. and Mouffe, C., 1985, *Hegemony and socialist strategy. Towards a radical democratic politics*, Verso, London.
50 See McCloskey, D., 2001, *Measurement and meaning in economics. The essential Deirdre McCloskey*, Edward Elgar, New York; Arndt, H.W., 1987, *Economic development. The history of an idea*, University of Chicago Press, Chicago; Samuels, W., 1990, *Economics as discourse*, Kluwer, Boston; Friman 2002; Gardiner, J., 1997, *Gender, care and economics*, Macmillan, London.
51 I disagree, for instance, with Jonas Hinnfors, who argues that social democracy has always been 'market-friendly'. Social democracy has 'always', with ups and downs, been a movement positively disposed to (regulated) capitalism, but the role of the market in how to create growth, and in actual fact the meaning of both 'growth' and 'market', is historically specific in modernisation discourses over time. See Hinnfors 2005.
52 Such continuities have been pointed out in the British case, where there were clear transfers of meaning between the post-fordist new times debate around *Marxism today* and the New Labour interpretation of modernisation. See Finlayson, A., 2003, *Making sense of New Labour*, p. 102f.
53 Pontusson, J., 1992, *The limits of social democracy. Investment politics in Sweden*, Cornell University Press, Ithaca; Benner, M., 1997, *The politics of growth. Economic regulation in Sweden 1930–1994*, Arkiv, Stockholm.
54 Boreus, K., 1994, *Högervåg*, Borea, Stockholm.
55 Lundberg-Petersen 1998 p. 104.
56 Ryner 2001.
57 Stråth 1998 p. 29.
58 Benner 1997 and Pontusson 1992 have made this point.
59 Therborn, G., 1983, '60–talet och den nya vänstern', in Vikström, L. (ed.), *Marx i Sverige*, Arbetarkultur, Lund; Östberg, K., 2003, *När allting var i rörelse. 60–talsradikaliseringen och de sociala rörelserna*, Prisma, Stockholm.

60 Ryner 2001.
61 Hall, P., 1993, 'Policy paradigms, social learning, and the state. The case of economic policymaking in Britain', *Comparative politics*, April, pp. 275–296.
62 Schön, D., 1993, 'Generative metaphor, a perspective on problem setting in social policy', in Ortony, A. (ed.), *Metaphor and thought*, Cambridge University Press, Cambridge; Williams, F., 2001, *Social policy – a critical introduction*, Polity, Cambridge.
63 See Searle, J., 1995, *The construction of social reality*, Penguin, London; Foucault, M., 1972, *The Archaeology of knowledge*, Routledge, London; Rueschemeyer, D. and Skocpol, T. (eds), 1996, *States, social knowledge and the origins of modern social policies*, Russell Sage Foundation/Princeton University Press, Princeton/New York.

2

A productive investment: social policy in the strong society

Introduction

In the immediate post-war period, economic growth became the obvious focus of politics. The modern concept of growth was born in the post-war debate on economic expansion. In the emergence of an international economic order following the reconstruction of European economies and the Marshall plan, the idea of development became redefined as *economic* development. The concept of growth, historically a metaphor that implied a balance between economic and social change and that saw economic change as an organic process, circumscribed by limits posed by social structures or the scarcity of resources, became reconceptualised as a question of virtually limitless industrial expansion. The very notion of progress became intrinsically linked to this idea of economic expansion. In the 1950s debate on poverty and inequality in expanding welfare capitalist economies of the West, as well in discussions on the developed and under-developed world, growth became the solution to all social evils. Ideas of growth contained hopes of a trickle-down process, by which growth would be disseminated to every segment of society.[1] To social democracy, growth became the promise of what Sassoon has called the growth consensus, as industrial growth seemed to make possible far-reaching social reform and redistribution without crippling class conflict.[2]

The introduction of the Bretton Woods-system in 1944 brought about the construction of an international standardised system for long-term economic planning, designed around the GDP concept as the quantitative measure of growth. In this process the concept of growth, and its quantitative definition as GDP, attained a hegemonic position also in national long-term planning. The modern concept of growth first appeared in Swedish planning in the third 5-year prognosis, the *långtidsutredning*, in 1955, which also introduced GDP as a statistical gauge of development.[3]

In the 1950s and 1960s the SAP went through a process of ideological rearticulation that has been described as social democracy's adaptation to the affluent society. This process of rearticulation centered on the demands and effects of industrial growth. The third generation of social democrats, lead by the minister of finance Gunnar Sträng, party leader Tage Erlander, and the minister of social affairs Sven Aspling, were faced with other problems than previous generations of the SAP. Previous party leaderships had been concerned with creating national unity, putting an economic framework in place, and relieving working class poverty. The people's home had now reached a certain maturity. Rising living standards in the booming Swedish post-war economy had brought about a 'middle-classification' of the working class that put pressure on social democracy's historical articulations of the interests of the working class, and challenged the SAP's role as the representative of those interests. The advancement of technology, mechanisation, and the pressures of a full employment economy required a more sophisticated analysis of the interplay between economic and social change than the party's 1930s articulations. [4]

This transition to a society characterised by affluence and improved living standards contained a certain ideological dilemma for the SAP. The people's home seemed to be more or less built, and yet social democracy had huge ambitions. The idea of the people's home as virtually finished was ideologically problematic. In the relatively consensus-tainted years of the early 1950s, the editor of the Liberal daily *Dagens Nyheter*, Hebert Tingsten, suggested polemically that the party leader Erlander would be the last social democrat standing, as social democracy had gradually reformed away its own class basis in the previous decades. Most groups in Swedish society lived in security. Tage Erlander himself was deeply troubled by this suggestion that society had in some way developed to the point of making social democracy redundant. The trouble in party debate in the mid 1950s was therefore how the SAP would rethink its role in an industrial society, where economic development seemed to bring about more security for all.[5]

In the election campaigns of the late 1950s, the slogan of 'the strong society' was coined as a way of facing up to this dilemma.[6] The slogan came about in coffee table discussions at the party headquarters in Sveavägen, suggested by the young aide to Erlander, Olof Palme. In his memoirs, the then party secretary Sven Aspling described the discussion where the concept was coined:

> We were sitting in Sveavägen this day discussing the themes of the electoral campaign ... At the party conference, Erlander confronted me: What do you think you're doing, my God, this is dynamite![7]

The metaphor of the strong society came to stand for a wide-reaching, collective responsibility for economic and social change, in order to steer change in the desired direction and make sure that groups weren't left behind in the process. Cornerstones of the ideology of the strong society were a rapidly-expanding public sector and an intensified economic policy to complete the structural transformation of Swedish society into a high-production industrial economy. The ideology of the strong society, as it took shape in a series of party programmes and reforms in the 1950s and early 1960s, was inherently optimistic. It placed its faith in the benefits of industrial capitalism and was confident in the capacity of social democracy to steer change towards the completion of its version of the socialist society, the welfare state. It drew on a notion of progress that can be described as linear, as progress was conceived of as an evolutionary and harmonious process whereby economic expansion would lead to increasing security and the fulfilment of ever more sophisticated social needs. The expansion of the public sector was conceptualised as an almost law-bound stage-driven process in tandem with industrial expansion. The conviction that economic development would continue to be favourable was obvious in the Labour movement's economic prognoses at the beginning of the 1960s.[8]

The prerequisite of this development was the SAP's ideological adherence to economic expansion and the needs of production. This was manifested in party ideology and rhetoric as a 'growth language', in which growth became the over-arching element in party ideology.[9]

The ideology of the strong society drew on the ideas of planning, *plan-hushållning*, that had been put forward by Wigforss's debate on rationalisation in the 1930s and further developed in the immediate post-war period. The doctrine of rationalisation that was the core of the Labour movement's post-war programme (*efterkrigsprogrammet*) stressed the need for economic and social planning in the industrial economy, in order to create a rational and efficient economy that could provide the economic resources for a continued expansion of the welfare state. Social intervention and far-reaching planning with social purposes were identified as central means for an efficient economy.[10] The strong society saw an increase in resources put into economic and social planning and a renewed emphasis on rationalisation. The bureaucracy of the welfare state grew substantially. In the mid-1950s, the postulates of the Rehn-Meidner model were drawn up. The Rehn-Meidner model's emphasis on structural change and labour mobility meant that the labour force came into focus as the central production factor.[11] The emphasis on planning and rationalisation of labour and social resources within the ideology of the strong society included a significant rise in social democracy's ambitions for groups that were previously on the fringes of social policy, and indeed in the margins of social democratic ideology. The strong society saw a fundamental change in social democracy's outlook on the role of social reform in the industrial society and new understandings of the notion of security. With the implementation of the big social insurance reforms of the mid-1950s, health insurance in 1955 and the pension reform (ATP) in 1959, most of the working population was incorporated into the welfare state. These reforms introduced the principle of income-related benefits and broke with the flat rate, general social policies of the 1930s. The creation of the pension reform following the strongly ideology-laden ATP conflict, that split the political spectrum, was a milestone for how the Labour movement thought about social reform in the twentieth century. Pensions for the working class were part of social democracy's historical agenda; until the first half of the twenty-first century their aim was to provide adequate living standards for the masses of the working class. Together with health insurance reform, ATP took universalism a step further by bringing the middle class into the welfare state.[12] In the transition between the 1950s and 1960s, the Labour movement's focus shifted from these large-scale social insurance reforms to social services and care within an expanding public sector. The focus on providing security in the form of material standards and income maintenance for the working and middle classes was broadened to include groups on the fringes of production, namely, women, the physically disabled, the elderly, the chronically ill, children and 'the asocial'. The notion of security came to encompass state responsibility for the adequate care of these groups. To increase the scope of social policies to target these groups, social services and social bureaucracy expanded considerably in the 1960s, and great demands were made on economic resources. Massive efforts were put into the education of social workers for the needs of local social bureaucracies.[13]

Rising expectations, security and freedom: social policy for a modern age

In a series of programmes in the late 1950s and early 1960s, the SAP set out a new role for social democracy that focused on the expansion of the public sector and on rising ambitions for groups still on the margins of the people's home. This process of rearticulation centered on a rethinking of the concept of security for a society of affluence. The notion of security that developed was intrinsically related to the idea of industrial growth.

Much of this process took place in the writings of the party leader Tage Erlander. In his treatises *Framstegens politik*, *Valfrihetens samhälle*, and *Människor i samverkan* (*The politics of progress*, *The society of freedom of choice*, and *People working together*), Erlander introduced a social democratic worldview in which industrial growth led to ever-increasing security for all, including society's vulnerable groups. Erlander saw industrial capitalism under the control of social democracy as a process of change that rapidly made destitution and poverty historic phenomena. Social problems, in Erlander's interpretation, were the remnants of an older stage of production and of a past of uncontrolled capitalist markets, and an anomaly within the social democratic society of planned growth and full employment. They would quickly disappear with the pace of progress. This interpretation of the historical character of social problems was strengthened by the abolition of poor relief in 1956 and its replacement with a new and modern social legislation that substituted the word for *poor relief* (*fattigvård*) with the word *social care* (*socialvård*). This was a reform measure with considerable symbolic importance for social democracy. Many leading social democrats had personal experience of poverty and the stigmatisation of poor relief. To Erlander, the abolition of the poor relief system was the final proof that social democratic policy had triumphed over 'poorhouse Sweden' (*Fattigsverige*). Universal social policies, as they had been formulated by the party in the 1930s, had fulfilled their task of eradicating poverty:

> The old society's feeble and far-too-often unwilling attitude to the destitute and the old was manifested in an institution that, beginning with its name, tormented and still torments many people, who remember this humiliation and poverty ... poor relief. Modern social policy has reduced poverty to a supplementary form of help for special cases – and by the end of the year, its name will disappear forever from our social legislation and be replaced by a modern, more humane form of social security.[14]

For Tage Erlander, however, this development did not mean that social democracy could sit back and relax. Social policy's tasks changed in the affluent society.

> Social policy's tasks will change. In a society of full employment, in which painful social need is an exception and where those with a reduced capacity for work can, little by little, be returned to a productive life and become self-supporting – in this society, the demands for security are ever more important.[15]

In the poor relief society, the role of social policy had been restricted to taking care of the infirm and weak groups outside of production. However, in a modern society with full employment, organised around economic growth and modern, rational production schemes, social policy should be in the 'service of progress', as an active part of the strong society's policies for continued economic and social development. The meaning of terms such as 'progress' and 'modern' in this discourse was derived from the link to production. In contrast to the old poor relief, modern social policies were reforms whose purpose was not only to provide relief for society's most vulnerable groups but to bring about their integration into production. The new social legislation in 1956 increased the level of ambition within social services dramatically. The objective of the new social legislation was formulated so as to 'bring back' (*återföra*) socially problematic individuals to production.[16] To Erlander, this reintegration into production would create security and freedom for single mothers and the physically disabled, elderly and sick, so that they could 'realise their dreams', make productive contributions and become part of the growth society. Modern social policies were modern because of their growth orientation.

This idea of the increased importance of social policy in the growth society was a way of refuting the liberal critique that security had reached a critical level in Swedish society, where the continued expansion of the public sector would be detrimental both to the economy and to individual freedom.[17] In contrast to the idea that social democracy had fulfilled its role in the process of change and that the welfare state was more or less completed, Erlander's rhetoric established the interpretation that security would only become more and more important in an industrial society. He argued that the abolition of destitution and the reduction of poverty to 'a problem of special cases' led not to a reduced importance for politics, but to new challenges for politics in terms of rising individual expectations on security and welfare. The rising standard of living meant that continually new and more demanding social needs would come into focus. It was first in the mature welfare state that the full range of social needs would become known. This interpretation found its expression early on in the rhetoric of Sven Aspling, who was appointed minister of health and social affairs in 1962, in his talks around the country:

> It is first in the welfare state that needs and shortages will become more immediately obvious. He who is secure wants more security ... In truth, we stand, not at the end of a reform era, but rather on the threshold of new tasks, new needs and emerging, urgent demands.[18]

Security was not something that could be finished, but rather demands for security expanded with economic expansion. Tage Erlander put words to this complex relationship with the notion of the revolution of rising expectations, or, as he put it, the disgruntlement of unfulfilled expectations. The meaning of this was that affluence lead to increasingly sophisticated social needs, needs that had to be fulfilled by the welfare state in order to maintain solidarity and public trust in politics. This discussion was clearly influenced both by Maslow's pyramid of social needs, and by the American economist John Kenneth Galbraith, whose book, *The affluent society,* greatly influenced the strong society's worldview.[19]

In this interpretation, the notion of security had to be expanded with the logic of industrial development, and the rate of growth had to be matched by increased public responsibility for individual wellbeing. This was the true meaning of the metaphor of the strong society. The continued expansion of social security in the industrial society was the prerequisite of individual freedom. In a society of rapid economic change, the emancipation of individuals was dependent on a social safety net that provided for freedom of choice, life chances and potential for all, including those particularly vulnerable to the process of change. The freedom of one depended on the solidarity of all. Security, to this extent, was the prerequisite of freedom. And to bring about individual freedom therefore required building a strong society. To that extent, the revolution of rising expectations encompassed a notion of security that meant that social democracy had to raise its ambitions regarding groups outside of production. No one could be left outside a strong society.

During the election campaigns of the late 1950s, this social democratic interpretation of the relationship between growth and security, and the importance of expanding public responsibility for economic and social development, was contrasted to the Liberal party's (*Folkpartiet*) articulations of the public sector's continued expansion as detrimental both to the economy and to individual freedom.[20] In 1962, Erlander talked of 'using willpower to build a new society'.[21] The needs of groups on the fringes of the labour market required considerable efforts on the part of society, involving the rehabilitation or 'return' of physically disabled and ill individuals to production; the expansion of childcare and care of the elderly to liberate women from the home; preventive measures for asocial individuals; and the expansion of treatment for alcoholics and youth welfare services. Some problems, for instance alcohol addiction and juvenile delinquency, seemed to be increasing in the growth society, a phenomenon that Erlander saw as 'in all likelihood ... related to the increased stress to which people are subjected in modern society', with its high production rate, technological advances and population resettlements in the wake of urbanisation. For Erlander, all of these were needs that must be fulfilled through greater responsibility for security and social welfare in an expanded public sector. The strong society required an expansion of social reform that would require considerable economic resources.[22]

> All of these things required single-minded measures from society's side, demands for an expansion of the public sector, demands that would inevitably be costly.[23]

For Tage Erlander, this expansion was neither an obstacle to economic development nor a limitation to indivual freedom but rather a condition for continued economic and individual growth.

The problem of left-over needs

The ideology of the strong society, however, was a tension-ridden one. This tension can be described as a vacillation between the emphasis on embarking on a new and radical project of building the strong society, and a more complacent attitude that saw security as an almost automatic process towards social harmony. In the election campaigns of the late 1950s, the Liberal party had spoken of 'silver polish' and there was something of this also in the rhetoric of the SAP. Despite Erlander's insistence that the importance of security was ever growing, there was a strong element in social democratic rhetoric that the most urgent social needs had been abolished and that what remained was mainly a question of the completion of the people's home. This created a strong tension in social democratic rhetoric between on the one hand emphasising its new and radical project of society-building and on the other falling back on a sometimes rather naïve faith in progress. This tension was strengthened by a very uncertain idea of social reality. The focus on social insurance reforms for the majority of the working class in the immediate post-war period had meant less attention for groups outside of the labour market, to the point that not much was known about them. Beneath the strong society's assertion that economic development would lead to the elimination of poverty and its substitution with more sophisticated social needs, there was therefore a degree of uncertainty as to what social needs actually still existed and which groups were left outside of the people's home, why this was and what would be required to integrate them. This insecurity was expressed in hesitant descriptions of social reality and in parliamentary questions such as *if* there actually were groups in Swedish society who were still living in poverty and what the possible reasons for this could be – statements that implied that there must be something fundamentally strange about such groups. In the late 1950s, a number of parliamentary communications were introduced on the issue of *whether* there were groups with 'special needs' in Sweden and if these could be 'cured' with modern social welfare. Was there still destitution and poverty in 'Welfare Sweden'?[24]

The emerging interest in these groups meant that considerable investments were made to increase knowledge about them. In the welfare state bureaucracy of the 1950s and 1960s, therefore, an intensive activity of knowledge-gathering and production of statistics regarding groups that might have fallen behind in the growth society began. In 1958, a large-scale social investigation, the Social Policy Committee, was charged with producing a comprehensive picture of the living conditions and needs of social groups in hospitals, elderly care, asylums and institutions around the country, and a study was initiated of low-wage groups in Swedish society.[25] This knowledge production produced an image of social reality that was strongly marked by the strong society's optimism and belief in the potential of growth to create increased security and bring about increased living standards for marginalised groups outside the labour market. The directives to the Social Policy Committee in 1958 included a clear perception of the nature of the social problem. The task of the Committee was defined as to map 'left-overs of economic hardship' and 'groups in need of special care from society'.[26] There was thus a clear idea that whatever problems still existed in the midst of Swedish society, they were either the remains of a previous era of material insecurity, or exceptions consisting of special needs or handicaps that fell outside of the traditional scope of reform politics. In the early years of the 1960s, the Social Policy Committee conducted an impressive number of investigations of groups and needs that could be categorised as 'special' – 'home daughters' (unmarried women taking care of elderly parents, often in the countryside), single mothers with children, the elderly in homes and institutions throughout the country, the physically disabled, hospital patients, the socially deviant and the asocial in asylums and mental hospitals.[27] The picture of the country's 'left-over needs' that emerged from this production of social statistics showed that the needy groups consisted of individuals who in the midst of full employment had remained outside of the labour force for a variety of reasons, and who were not able to keep up with the pace of change. Their living standard was significantly lower than the average Swede's. 'Special needs' however, was an elastic term. The Low-Income Study identified a rather impressive group of 692,000 individuals with significantly low incomes. In addition to this big group of people who had somehow been left behind with regard to solidary wages and full employment, there were signs that some problems, primarily 'asocial developments', including alcoholism, juvenile delinquency and the early stages of substance abuse, had increased dramatically in the recent period.[28]

Thus, this knowledge production presented a picture of social reality that seemed to comprise great and even growing social needs. However, the interpretation of the causality behind this image of social reality in the final report of the Social Policy Committee was utterly in line with the strong society's worldview of increasing security in the industrial society. The metaphor of 'left-over needs' that had steered the directives to the Committee, came to steer also its conclusion of the nature of the policy problem. The Social Policy Committee stated that the expansion of social services and the increased public responsibility for individual security through the public sector was a new stage in the transformation of Swedish society. The roots of this transformation were growth, increased employment outside of the home for women, and the transfer of individuals from the countryside to cities and industrial centres by the politics of mobility. Mobility had made groups in need of care more vulnerable. The breakup of the family structure and the 'the flight from the country' related to the intense structural change of the period had left the elderly and physically disabled alone. Urbanisation had caused problems of delinquency and alcoholism. From the viewpoint of personal security, this was a 'negative side of development'. However, the Social Policy Committee stated, since society had accepted the consequences of this change in terms of a relocation of responsibility from the personal to the public sphere, the Committee was not negatively disposed to these developments. It dismissed these problems as being of a passing nature. The predominant interpretation of the Committee was that this process of change would also permit the vulnerable groups to take part in the increased material prosperity that change brought about. Also, those negatively affected by change would in time reap its benefits, and become 'competitive consumers' along with the rest of the working class.[29] This framing of the social problem as something that would gradually evaporate with the continued expansion of production shaped the Committee's perception of the necessary problem-solving. The Committee's main proposal was a new role for social policy in the form of an active social policy that sought out individuals and groups outside the labour market in order to integrate them in production. Such a policy would be in keeping with the goals of the social legislation of 1956, and in the view of the Committee, active social policy heralded the definitive end to the poor relief epoch.[30]

Such active social policies were also part of the 'total engagement in production' required to bring about security for these groups. A total engagement in production required a change in society's attitude towards the socially needy. A society with full employment must take complete responsibility for the labour force and assume responsibility for the groups in need of care. This interpretation of the mechanisms behind increased social needs in an industrial society became the predominant one, in spite of the fact that the committee also believed that economic development and structural transformation were directly responsible for what they did see as a significant increase in individual insecurity. Growth created security. In the social planning of the strong society, therefore, a perfectly coherent worldview emerged, according to which economic expansion led to an increase in demands for security, but the fulfilment of those demands was a productive measure aimed at including previously passive social groups in production.

Growth created security, but security was also given a clear role for creating growth. The political commitment to full employment and industrialisation had created the need for an accessible labour force, and this need was a major motivation for an expansion of social policy. Policies aimed at the integration of these groups into production were a productive form of social policy.[31] Security, then, also created growth.[32]

Social policy and the Rehn-Meidner model

At the heart of the idea of the strong society, then, was the conception that economic and social progress went hand in hand. Growth led to increasing security, but the continued expansion of security was also a precondition for further economic expansion. Thus, the strong society's raised ambitions in the social sphere were based on the understanding that social and economic advances were dependent on one another. Rising ambitions for the social services' groups were motivated in relation to understandings of the needs of production and the need for a full commitment to the productive economy. This meant that social policy was given a direct relationship to economic policy, and the expansion of social policy and the public sector occupied a central place in the Labour movement's economic discourse.

As the Rehn-Meidner model was drawn up in the economic policy programmes of the SAP and the trade union federation, the LO, in the 1950s and 1960s, social policy was given a specific role, alongside active labour market policies, to target labour reserves and include 'remaining groups' outside the labour market into production.[33] The productivism and supply side orientation of the Rehn-Meidner model is well known. In the mid 1950s, the LO had taken on the economy's structural issues. The postulates of the Rehn-Meidner model included a compehensive trade union responsibility for structural change, by solidary wage bargaining that would keep wages at a level sufficiently high to push low wage sectors out of the economy, and by accepting the mobility of active labour market policies that would shift labour to high productive industrial sectors in urban areas. The trade union movement, thus, wholeheartedly accepted modernisation as something that would benefit its members. The prerequisite for this was in many ways the idea that an extended public responsibility would protect the individual worker from the negative effects of mobility, and the expansion of a social safety net that in the form of both social insurances and social services would guarantee material security in times of transition and temporary need. This was in Swedish discourse codified as 'security in change' (*trygghet i förändring*).[34]

The general guidelines for the economic policy of the 1960s were drawn up in a report by the Economic Policy Committee to the 1961 Swedish Trade Union Confederation Congress (LO), entitled *Samordnad näringspolitik* (*Coordinated economic policy*). Together with this report and the document *Resultat och reformer* (*Results and reforms*), formulated by the SAP and the LO in 1964, the groundwork was laid for an economic policy that included a highly growth-oriented or productivist approach to society and economy, and that established a discourse around social policy as a central means for growth. This economic discourse set growth and security as objectives in utter harmony, and it denied that there could conceivably be any conflict between them in the process of modernisation.[35]

At the beginning of the 1960s, there was a growing debate in the Labour movement on possible harmful effects of structural change on the social sphere, and there was also a growing awareness of the effects of industrial capitalism on the environment. There were suggestions that the growth rate and living standards had reached a level where the Labour movement could afford to attach less importance to demands for economic effectiveness and move on to less material values. *Coordinated economic policy* acknowledged this growing debate on the social limits of industrial capitalism and an internal party critique of 'technocratic ideals of efficiency', but it dismissed this criticism as fatally misconstrued. *Coordinated economic policy* insisted that only through continued economic expansion would it be possible to create resources for the continued expansion of the welfare state and the reforms in social services planned. Growth and the continued expansion of production were the basis for continued social progress for meeting the considerable social needs that existed in the public sector and for proceeding with social democratic efforts to create security. Social democratic values of security, equality and freedom required a growing 'material foundation'. To realise those values, future economic policies of the Labour movement must concentrate on expansion and increased productivity. The creation of security demanded full support for rationalisation and intensified structural overhaul of the Swedish economy, and the first priority of the Labour movement had to be growth.[36]

The report thus laid down the need for continued growth. Moreover it rejected the idea that one could relate processes of industrial rationalisation to signs of insecurity, psychological stress or other 'syndromes' in the growth society. In the view of *Coordinated economic policy,* a certain degree of insecurity was a 'necessary consequence' of thoroughgoing structural change, but in all likelihood such consequences would be temporary. In the long term, the economic and social goals would merge into 'one goal – a better society'. Accordingly, possible negative social consequences of the politics of mobility were deemed as being of a passing nature on the way from a less efficient society to a highly productive industrial economy. Economic effectiveness created security and there was no conflict between objectives of growth and objectives of individual security.[37]

In the same way, security, through the expansion of the public sector, created economic effectiveness. The report argued that this had to be the social democratic definition of change. It was a bourgeois conception that security and effectiveness could be posited against one another. In actual fact, the development of social policy was a core instrument for mobility and continued productivity expansion, and the challenge for the 1960s was to strengthen the interplay between economic and social policy. The central message of *Coordinated economic policy* was that objectives of growth, on the one hand, and objectives of individual security, on the other, had to be increasingly coordinated. It argued that the reform process in the post-war period had occurred without sufficient coordination. The social reforms carried out by the Labour movement had been too motivated by social concerns and had not sufficiently taken overarching economic objectives into account. The continued reform process and the public sector's expansion must be devised, therefore, as part of a coordinated economic policy for structural change. The protection of vulnerable groups must not be allowed to impede on continued rationalisation by decreasing labour mobility or putting a hold on productivity by subsidising a labour force that remained in the countryside or in insufficient employment. Thus, the expansion of social services was understood as a vital tool for effective production and the rational management of production resources, and they must be made part of an overall economic strategy. Coordinated economic policy meant increased concertation between economic and social policy.[38]

Social balance and productive consumption

In this social democratic language of rationalisation, mobility, and structural transformation, individual security was increasingly related to the needs of production, and social policy became conceptualised as an investment into the productive economy and a facilitator of structural change. To this extent the ideology of the strong society drew on the 1930s discussion on the productive role of social policy. This notion of investment was central to the Labour movement's outlook on the strategic role of the expansion of the public sector. The idea of the famous Swedish 'middle way' was that the mixed economy (*blandekonomi*) consisted of an ideal balancing of public and private, where the public sector provided for industry by catering for consumption needs that had crucial spillover effects on industry, but would not be fulfilled by the market to the detriment of the economy as a whole. This was strongly related to an idea of public and social good; that there were social needs whose fulfilment represented a wider social good and had indispensable effects on societal efficiency. In the Labour movement's 1960s economic language, this productivist attitude towards social policy was expressed in social democratic rhetoric through the use of metaphors such as 'social balance', 'productive consumption' and 'social investment', to describe the productive character of the resources put into the public sector.

Coordinated economic policy carried on a long discussion of the term 'social balance'. In the report, the concept of social balance was used to designate consumer needs whose fulfilment represented a public good that had to be catered for by an expansion of public responsibility. There were increased demands for social services, childcare and rehabilitation – things that would have productive effects on the labour force but that were not provided for by the private sector at reasonable cost. Through a growing public sector, demand could be directed towards economically productive social needs and consumption be steered towards public goods. The LO, therefore, wholeheartedly supported a rapid expansion of the public sector as a vital component in a strategy for increased overall productivity.

> This means that we accept the continued strong growth of the public sector's role in our economy. Such growth is much more justifiable, as those needs that would be satisfied many times over are much more important for society than are large segments of private consumption.[39]

The concept of social balance was borrowed from J.K. Galbraith and *The affluent society.* In his book, Galbraith made a plea for the strategic importance of public consumption in societies characterised by affluence. Galbraith's discussion on class dynamics in an industrial society was based on the observation that there seemed to be no tendencies in industrial society towards increased equality. Rather, affluence was increasingly unevenly redistributed. Growth did not 'trickle down'. Affluence had provided scope for an expansion of private consumption that lead to widening class divisions. Galbraith based this conclusion on his observations of American urban poverty, which appeared to be accelerating in spite of strong growth. Some groups seemed to be permanently left behind and marginalised in industrial society. Galbraith's idea of 'social balance' required that growth be directed towards public consumption that would also benefit these groups. He advocated that growth be increasingly guided towards public consumption in order to refute this development and steer consumption towards a wider social good.

Galbraith's ideas fit in well with the SAP's idea of the strong society. They were quite consistent with Tage Erlander's discussion on the changing role of social democratic politics in the growth society, the growing demand for security and an increased collective responsibility vis-à-vis the neglected groups in society.[40] There was however an important difference between the reception of Galbraith's book in the US and its reading by Swedish Social Democracy. In the US, *The affluent society* was read as a critique of the growth society. Galbraith's idea of urban poverty as something that grew and worsened in the midst of affluence triggered a renewed discourse on inequality and poverty in the American left. Swedish social democracy, however, read Galbraith's book as a defence of its interpretation of the dynamics of the growth society. Galbraith's ideas strengthened the SAP's interpretation that an industrial society required a high degree of planning and public responsibility, but that growth, in a socialist economy, was a wider social good. Social balance, in the interpretation of the SAP, became a concept that stood for the role of the public sector in a strategy for growth, but it never questioned the class dynamics of the affluent society nor the idea that growth would, in a social democratic society, lead to the benefit of all.

This approach to the economically favourable effects of public consumption as a core element of national efficiency and an investment into the economy as a whole permeated economic planning in the 1960s, and it took expression in a series of debates around the accurate definition of concepts of production and consumption in the Swedish mixed economy, which essentially denied that there was any significant difference between these when it came to public expenditure.

The concept of GDP was introduced into Swedish long-term economic planning in 1955 with great scepticism. The understanding of efficiency that it conveyed did not fit Swedish understandings of the intricate balance between public and private, or between a productive economy on the one hand and social efficiency on the other. The five-year prognosis that introduced the concept included a lengthy discussion of its shortcomings as a statistical gauge for societal development and progress in general and as a measure of the productive effects of public consumption in particular.[41] The main problem was that GDP did not measure any qualitative aspects of social progress in terms of the ways in which economic expansion affected individual security or living standards – issues that Swedish planning considered to be at the core of policymaking. The measure of GDP meant a narrow focus on economic development that was not in line with Swedish understanding of efficiency as a question of social balance or social efficiency, *samhällsekonomisk effektivitet*. Further, among the drawbacks of GDP as a planning tool was the fact that its gauge of productivity was restricted to measuring productivity in those services that were traded on a market with a price mechanism. This left out the public sector. By definition, international GDP measures set the productivity of public sectors to zero or close to zero. This meant that the national product did not reflect the real value of the public sector's production or the economic effects of the considerable investments undertaken in social reform in Swedish society.[42] In the Swedish debate it was therefore argued that the concept was particularly unsuitable for Swedish purposes. The Swedish economy was dominated by a rapidly expanding public sector, and Swedish politics were marked by the ambition to further increase this, largely because of concerns with growth. Moreover, values surrounding public consumption in Sweden differed from policy ambitions in other countries where public expenditure was not given the same strategic role for economic and social progress. The concept, after all, was an American invention, created to fit a market capitalist understanding of economy and society. In Swedish long-term planning in the mid-1950s, it was concluded, therefore, that GDP was an insufficient index of production. GDP was a measure that was, by and large, 'arbitrarily constructed' and with a 'limited range', since it excluded economic effects that in Swedish economic policy had been determined as vital for the productive expansion of the economy and continued growth. The GDP measure failed to provide an accurate account of a central policy problem, namely the productive effects of the public sector. As the concept was nevertheless reluctantly introduced into Swedish policymaking for reasons of international harmonisation, a debate started that would go on in Swedish politics throughout the post-war period. This debate began in the observation that GDP was insufficient for assessments of the role of the public sector in the economy and that GDP was insufficient as a reliable basis for strategic policy decisions concerning the public sector, but it also identified the need for better methods for measuring productivity in the public sector as one of economic planning's most important tasks.[43] This search for better measures of the public sector's role in the economy would go on in economic planning throughout the 1960s, 1970s and 1980s and reflect the shifting understandings of the public sector's role in the economy of each time.

This rejection of what in Swedish discourse was dubbed the zeroing (*nollning*) of public sector productivity in GDP is a clear indication of the assumption in

Swedish economic planning that public consumption has central productive effects, even if these were difficult to measure. This assumption became clear in the language and metaphors surrounding the expansion of the public sector, particularly in the five-year prognoses. In subsequent economic planning in the 1960s, expansion of the public sector and social services was discussed in terms of an economic investment. With metaphors such as 'productive consumption' and 'expenditures for the future acquisition of revenues', public consumption was defined as a central investment into the economy, equal in comparison to other productive activities of the national economy. From these perspectives, the distinction between consumption and production became blurred. In 1960, the five-year prognosis argued that even if the expansion of social services formally represented consumption, it must be taken into account on the production side of the economy, since it constituted the prerequisite for continued expansive production. They were investments with a specific consumer motivation, and investments that supported production in both the short and the long term.[44] This outlook came to the fore when, in 1965, the expansion of public consumption led to some unrest in economic planning with inflationary pressure, and it was suggested that the public sector might be crowding out private consumption and the economic space for investments in trade and industry. The five-year prognosis was the first to suggest that maybe the expansion of the public sector should be slowed down. The Minister of Finance Gunnar Sträng then intervened to stress that public consumption could not be viewed simply as consumption. The expansion of the public sector fulfilled social needs that had economically favourable consequences, for example, in the form of increased opportunities for individuals to take part in production. Therefore, public consumption could not be weighed against private consumption or the need to invest in trade and industry. According to Sträng, public consumption was, in fact, characterised by its ability to 'represent consumption and production at the same time'. 'Like investments in fixed capital', resources for the public sector increased production, and expenditures for consumption that expanded opportunities for individuals to participate in production should be regarded as 'productive investments'.[45]

Labour reserves and production factors

In social democratic economic discourse, then, a discourse on social policy took shape that defined social policy as a productive investment into the industrial economy. 'Investment' became an organising metaphor for economic and social reform. The notion of investment set in place a particular framework around social policy, and also coloured the SAP's outlook on the groups within social policy, such as the remaining poor, the disabled, the elderly, women and the 'asocial'; groups that were now constructed as potential production factors and labour market reserves. The central role of social policy was identified in the freeing up of a labour reserve in social services, thereby putting all available labour resources into production. Rehabilitation, re-education and childcare were identified as investments in the labour force and thereby as productive expenditures. Within the Rehn-Meidner model, social policy was given a strong relationship to active labour market policy as a central means for the allocation of labour resources and for increasing the value of labour. Social policy was identified as a vehicle for increasing labour mobility and labour productivity, for putting potential labour force reserves to work, including 'underused groups' and groups 'difficult to place', and for investing in the labour force as a core production factor through care and services. Social and demographic planning was considered an important means by which one could monitor changes in the supply of social resources, and activate and allocate all available labour assets.[46] In the government bill for active labour market policies, all socially problematic groups were placed in the labour reserve: mentally ill individuals and those with learning disabilities, the physically disabled, the hearing- and visually-impaired, those with TB, the socially maladjusted, alcoholics and people previously deemed too old to work. They were all part of an underused resource who could now contribute productively to society. The proposal for active labour market policies was coupled with an increased emphasis on rehabilitation and activation, applied not only to physically disabled and those injured at work, but to all 'potentially able-bodied individuals' including people who were work-inhibited, negatively disposed to society as a whole, or who had been 'socially damaged' following years of confrontation with the institutions of the welfare state. The costs for this rehabilitation were economically defendable because of the productive effect on potential labour force resources. Rehabilitation created 'its own economic foundation'.[47]

Concluding remarks

The ideology of the strong society has been described in the previous pages as a social democratic worldview, where economic and social advances drew on each other, and where the expansion of security was inextricably related to industrial expansion. Growth, under the control of democratic socialism, was identified as the primary means for social development and increased security, and as a means that would, in the near future, overcome the evils of capitalism and spread affluence to all groups in society. Security, on the other hand, was articulated as a precondition for a productive economy; the lubricant of the process of modernisation towards the advanced industrial economy. To this extent, the strong society was a coherent worldview, where economic expansion and individual security coexisted in utter harmony. Its commitment to progress in the form of a highly productive economy was based on this faith in a balanced development.

This, then, was a notion of progress that saw change as a fundamentally unproblematic process that led towards the completion of the people's home. The role of politics within this framing was to steer change towards the fulfilment of individual and public good. However, the strong society was also an inherently economistic ideology, one in which social goals seemed to derive their meaning from the economic. The strong society's interest in groups outside of the labour market was motivated by its conception of the pace of production as the fundamental driver of social change, a driver that under social democratic control would work for the better of all. Its equalisation of economic expansion with progress, and its belief that social problems were rooted in older stages of capitalism and shaped its ideas of social reality, were central – to the point that signs that seemed to indicate tensions between productive expansion and individual security were excluded from ideology; silenced as temporary glitches in the process of creating a more efficient society. These tensions would come to the surface in the following decade.

Notes

1 Friman 2002 pp. 62, 100–124; Arndt 1987 p. 49f.
2 Sassoon 1996.
3 Friman 2002 pp. 45, 49; SOU 1956:53.
4 See Levin, L., 1967, *Planhushållningsdebatten*, Tiden, Stockholm; Esping-Andersen 1985.
5 See Ruin, O., 1986, *I välfärdsstatens tjänst. Tage Erlander 1946–1969*, Tiden, Stockholm; Erlander, T., 1982, *1960–talet*, Tiden, Stockholm; Erlander, T., 1975, *Tage Erlander: 1949–1954*, Tiden, Stockholm.
6 Ruin 1986 p. 233; Aspling, S., 1999, *Med Erlander och Palme*, Tiden, Stockholm, p. 116f.
7 Aspling 1999 p. 116: '*Vad är det ni håller på med, herre gud, det här är ju dynamit rakt igenom!*' I have shortened the original quote slightly.
8 Johansson-Magnusson 1998 p. 45; Erlander, T., 1962, *Valfrihetens samhälle*, Tiden, Stockholm.
9 Stråth 1998 pp. 69–94. Cf. Sassoon 1996.
10 Tilton 1991.
11 Lewin 1967 p. 437; Benner 1997 p. 96f; Olsson 1994.
12 Heclo-Madsen 1987; Olsson, S., 1990, *Social policy and welfare state in Sweden*, Arkiv, Lund.
13 Olsson 1990; SOU 1966:13.
14 Erlander, T., 1956, *Framstegens politik*, Tiden, Stockholm, p. 34.
15 Ibid.
16 Holgersson, L., 1997, *Socialpolitik och socialt arbete*, Norstedts Juridik, Stockholm, pp. 50–53.
17 See Ohlin, B., 1975, *Bertil Ohlins memoarer 1940–1951. Socialistisk skördetid kom bort*, Bonnier, Stockholm.
18 Sven Aspling speech, Bommersvik, August 5 1964, in Sven Aspling's archives.
19 Galbraith, J.-K., 1958, *The affluent society*, Prisman, Stockholm. Galbraith's book was published in Swedish by the Labour movement publishing house Tiden with the title *Överflödets samhälle* in 1959.
20 See Liberal party, *Folkpartiet, Världen och vi på 1960–talet.*
21 Erlander 1962 p. 31.
22 Erlander 1954 p. 17, 1962 p. 44f.
23 Erlander 1962 p. 31.
24 Sven Aspling speech, *Träindustriarbetareförbundet*, September 8 1963, in Sven Aspling's archives; parliament bill [*riksdagens skrivelse*] 1958:78 and 1956:176; SOU

1964:59.
25 *1959 års Socialhjälpsundersökning* p. 11; *Lågainkomsttagarundersökningen*, SOU 1964:59, appendix 3.
26 SOU 1964:59 p. 81.
27 SOU 1961:38; SOU 1963:47; SOU 1964:5; SOU 1964:43; SOU 1964: 59.
28 *1959 års Socialhjälpsundersökning* p. 70f.; SOU 1964:43 pp. 34–43; SOU 1964:59 pp. 87–97; SOU 1967:36 pp.19, 41.
29 SOU 1966:45 p. 21.
30 SOU 1966:45 pp. 9–15, 117.
31 SOU 1966:45 p. 20f; SOU 1964:59 p. 29.
32 SOU 1964:43 p. 15.
33 LO-SAP 1964, *Resultat och reformer* (Results and reform); SOU 1965:9, *Arbetsmarknadsutredningen*, Stockholm.
34 Benner 1997.
35 Stråth 1998 p. 76; LO, 1961, *Samordnad näringspolitik*; cf. LO 1951, *Fackföreningsrörelsen och den fulla sysselsättningen*, and LO-SAP 1964.
36 LO 1961 pp. 37, 48, 63, 65, 149.
37 LO 1961 p. 37.
38 Ibid.
39 LO 1961 p. 35.
40 See Erlander 1962 p. 60 and Tilton 1990 pp. 166–188, for the concept of social balance; O'Connor 2001 p. 146f.
41 SOU 1956:53 p. 13.
42 SOU 1956:53 p. 37f.
43 SOU 1956:53 p. 39.
44 SOU 1962:10 p.133.
45 SOU 1966:13 p. 48
46 LO 1961 p. 151; SAP-LO 1964 p. 29.
47 SOU 1964:51 pp. 25, 74; SOU 1965:9, pp. 342, 526; government bill 1966:52; SOU 1961:29; SOU 1964:51; SOU 1964:43 p. 8.

3

The social cost of growth

Introduction

In the late 1960s, the strong society's optimistic idea of ever-increasing security in industrial society clashed with new images of reality, which focused on extensive social problems in the midst of social democratic society.

In 1967, the husband and wife team of Gunnar and Maj Inghe published *Den ofärdiga välfärden* (*Unfinished welfare*), a book about the social welfare clientele in Stockholm.[1] Gunnar Inghe was a professor of social medicine who had conducted several investigations into marginalised social groups and the labour reserves in the 1960s. *Unfinished welfare* was a fitting title, one that was in direct conflict with the social democratic rhetoric of 'left-over needs' and an almost finished welfare state. The welfare state was not at all complete. *Unfinished welfare* started a heated debate on the shortcomings of social democratic policy in the post-war period, a debate that quickly intensified as more reports targeted the shortcomings of the people's home from a wide range of perspectives. A survey on the treatment of alcoholism concluded that social legislation was, in actual fact, a class legislation aimed at vulnerable workers. While drunken company directors enjoyed treatment in expensive clinics, working class alcoholics were picked up by police and put in social care.[2] In 1966, an LO report on the work environment had shocked many Social Democrats with its description of exposed industrial workers in heavily mechanised industrial environments, and in the following year a government committee, the Committee on Low Income, began to produce statistics that pointed to large groups of people within extremely low income levels despite full employment and solidary wage bargaining. These extremely low wage earners existed between social services and the labour market, and seemed to have been increasingly marginalised as the pace of production picked up in the 1950s and early 1960s. In the face of the optimistic post-war view on harmonious social and economic development, these new images of social reality led to the interpretation that growth had not, in fact, spread to all groups in society; instead, it had created new social problems. An intense debate on post-war social democratic policy and the role of social democracy in an industrial society began. This debate quickly focused on the concept of social exclusion.

This chapter deals with the period spanning the late 1960s and early 1970s as a period of critique in which the relationship between social reality and social democratic ideology was fundamentally questioned. This late 1960s debate was a major break with the relative consensus around social policy in the late 1950s and early 1960s, and social policy, particularly the policies directed at groups within social welfare and social services, became a core ideological issue for the SAP.

Knowledge production from technocratic reform to critique

The Swedish version of '1968' has been described as a critique of reformism from within the left fringes of social democracy. Armed with the analytical tools of critical sociology and heavily influenced by Marxism and radical social work, groups in the administration of the welfare state called into question the organisation of welfare and security within the framework of the capitalist system.[3] In a sense, this development stood in continuity with the ideas of the strong society. The strong society's rising social ambitions and its position on eradicating left-over needs led to considerable investments in increased knowledge on social reality and a major expansion of social administration, planning and research. In the rationalist and pragmatic political culture of the Swedish model, social reform was inherently technocratic, with policymakers defining the nature of the social problem for empirical social science to solve. Sociology became a discipline at the service of the welfare state, as huge resources were put into the education of social workers and large scale social investigations. The late 1960s changed this power relationship between politics and social science.[4] At the end of the 1960s the strong society's search for knowledge about social reality resulted in images of reality that did not correspond to its worldview. These displacements in the relationship between reality and ideology resulted in a struggle in which the signs of increasing social problems that had been excluded from the strong society's ideology gradually came to the surface in a growing critique of the SAP and social policy. In this process, actors deeply involved in the strong society's knowledge production made their appearance as groups struggling for authoritative the power to define the social policy problem. These groups occupied a space between planning and debate. From being part of the knowledge production of the strong society in the post-war period, they now turned on social democratic policy and ideology.

The Association of Directors of Swedish Social Welfare Services (*Föreningen Sveriges socialchefer,* hereafter the social workers or FSS), which consisted of professional social workers and directors of the local social policy boards, had been in existence since the 1930s; however, the association experienced a huge upswing in its activities during the period 1967–72, concurrently with the radicalisation of the debate and the parallel professionalisation of social workers. During these years, its annual seminars turned into noteworthy phenomena that brought together large segments of the public debate in discussions of social policy and its role in the capitalist society. Over time, there was a marked escalation of the social workers' discourse. In 1966, 1967 and 1968, the FSS's seminars concentrated on issues of methodology in social work, the design of social services and details in social legislation.[5] But in 1969, 1970 and 1971, they escalated into a critique of the market economy and the subordination of social policy to economic policy in the Swedish 'middle way' model.

The social workers drew inspiration from the work of the Committee on Low Income. This committee was appointed by the social democratic government after initial findings in the mid-1950s seemed to indicate growing social needs and the existence of remaining poverty in a significantly large group in Swedish society. The directive to the Committee on Low Income was to find out why a large group of people seemed to be in need of social assistance and living in poverty in spite of growth, full employment, and solidary wage bargaining. The directives hinted that this must be rooted in individual causes and personal circumstance, but they also expressed a dawning fear that 'more universal conditions' had something to do with it.

> There is a pressing need to obtain a better understanding of why many citizens in a society with full employment cannot escape less profitable or unstable jobs for ones that are more lucrative.[6]

The Committee on Low Income rapidly became one of the most vocal critics of the SAP. Like the social workers, it took a position between the knowledge production in the administration of the welfare state and the public debate. Its findings were disseminated in a series of debate books published by members of the Committee as well as by the Social Democratic Youth and the LO, the Trade Union Federation.[7] Over time, the Committee became increasingly radical. This radicalisation was largely due to its young secretary, the LO economist Per Holmberg. Holmberg, who was one of the more prominent figures of the Swedish new left and was to play a leading role in the critique of the SAP, took over much of the Committee's work from its Chair, Rudolf Meidner, one of the architects of the famous Rehn-Meidner model that laid the foundations for much of post-war economic and social policy.[8] Along with Holmberg, a number of other young economists in the LO's Economic department intervened in the debate and directed strong criticism towards social democracy and the economic policies of the post-war period, to the extent that they turned on many of the post-war policies that had originated in the same LO department in the 1950s and early 1960s, and indeed on the postulates of the Rehn-Meidner model.[9]

The problem of social exclusion

Social workers and LO economists rapidly defined the problem as a problem of social exclusion. This was a formulation of the social policy problem that differed considerably from the strong society's definition of social problems as a question of 'left-over needs'. Whereas the meaning of the metaphor of 'left-over needs' clearly was that social problems were remnants of an older production order and something that would in time disappear with the expansion of industrial growth and the completion of the social democratic welfare state, the metaphor of 'social exclusion' conjured up an image of social problems as created by growth, and, more precisely, by the productivist orientation of the SAP's post-war policies.

The preliminary findings of the Committee on Low Income in 1968 and 1969 indicated a segregated social services and low-income group consisting of individuals who, for a variety of reasons, were vulnerable in the industrial society: women, the handicapped, the sick and the old, but also a number of people in the working class, who suffered from what the Committee defined as extremely low income. To an extent, the Committee found that the reasons were 'universal', depending on sickness or periodic unemployment. But the Committee also identified a major cause of poverty in the systematic disposal and exhaustion of individuals, following problems such as poor working conditions, weariness from rationalisation and mechanisation and increased insecurity on the heels of structural change. The politics of mobility of the Rehn-Meidner model had displaced great numbers of the working class from agrarian areas to rapidly expanding suburbs in the cities of Stockholm, Malmö and Göteborg, causing, in the Committee's interpretation, fundamental alienation and a widespread feeling of rootlessness. Moreover, the Committee identified a crucial factor of poverty in conditions that affected the individual from birth, in a 'social heritage' that seemed to reproduce social marginalisation from generation to generation. The committee concluded that social democratic redistribution and welfare policy had not decreased class distinctions and insecurities and that there was a sizeable group of poor workers who had been born into misfortune and further, were worn out because of post-war production changes.[10]

Much of this discussion was reminiscent of the debate that started in the US after the publication of Michael Harrington's book *The other America* in 1964. Harrington described a development in American society wherein social problems seemed to be inherited from one generation to the next, resulting in an underclass of permanently marginalised poor. In the following years, the American debate focused on the idea a culture of poverty, caused by welfare dependency and passivity. It saw social exclusion and the new underclass as phenomena rooted, ultimately, in individual shortcomings and a culture of poverty, where values of dependency were transmitted from generation to generation.[11]

The Swedish debate had certain similarities, particularly in the way that the concept of social exclusion came to encompass a large group of people who were not only materially poor but who also suffered from what the Committee on Low Income termed political poverty, or the lack of political resources, and who were thus 'outsiders' to the social and political world and had no possibility of changing their own situation.[12] The idea of a social heritage was central to this, as it seemed to pinpoint a social phenomenon that was not a question of things that could be directly remedied through policies targeted at income levels and so forth, but, rather, was a question of birth and upbringing. The differences in the Swedish interpretation of the concept of social exclusion or indeed of an underclass from its the American discourse, were, however, substantial. The Swedish debate insisted that social exclusion was a structural problem and not something that had roots in individual failure or individual attitudes. The metaphor used to denote exclusion in Swedish, *utslagning*, is indicative. Originally a sports metaphor used for instance in boxing, *utslagning* literally means 'struck out' and necessarily draws the attention to the agent that strikes out. The Swedish debate, moreover, quickly targeted politics as the key cause of social exclusion. The 'underclass' was politically created, and, in particular, it had been created by the growth orientation of the SAP.

The definition of the problem of social exclusion fell back on a concept of security that was much wider than the notion of security that had laid the foundation for social policy in the strong society. This reconceptualisation was made possible by the theoretical notion of 'living standard' and the statistical measure of living standard components which was the basis for the work of the Committee on Low Income. This was mainly developed by the sociologist Sten Johansson. The living standard concept was formulated as a statistical gauge of qualitative changes in security and insecurity. It consisted of nine components that would cover an individual's entire living situation, from nutritional intake and conditions during one's youth to working environment. 'Security', in this understanding, was not just a matter of income or consumption opportunities but rather one of an individual's total living environment and general welfare.[13] In the discourse on social exclusion, the living standard concept became a key metaphor, one that made new framings of the social problem possible by, first of all, permitting new statistical descriptions of reality, and secondly, by providing theoretical input for how to interpret them and define what was wrong. In this way, the concept enabled the critique to go from statistical descriptions of low wages and social needs to an understanding of social exclusion as something that fundamentally challenged the strong society's ideology and required a dramatically different method of social problem-solving.

The Committee on Low Income produced an impressive collection of statistical surveys and discussions, but it never prepared its last report, which was to have summarised the Swedish people's living conditions; instead, its findings were issued in a series of memoranda and chapter outlines, since the work of the 1971 committee was discontinued when Olof Palme shut the investigation down. The final conclusion of the report was therefore published not as a government committee report but as a pamphlet issued by the LO's Economic department to the 1971 LO congress, entitled *Låglön och välfärd* (*Low wages and welfare*).[14]

Low wages and welfare was written as a blistering condemnation of the strong society's ideology and the Rehn-Meidner model. The complicated statistical results of the Committee on Low Income were illustrated graphically with an ominous image of the dynamics of social exclusion, where the components of the living standard measure added up to a spider web that trapped the individual in vicious circles of exclusion over the life cycle. The report concluded that social democratic policy was the source of systematic exclusion of society's weak groups. Social democracy had failed to uphold the values of socialism; rather, it had recreated capitalism in the form of a specific variant that the report entitled 'social democratic capitalism'. The class society had not been abolished, but the 'capitalist hydra' had acquired a new head.[15] The class structure of this new labour-led capitalist order was, however, strikingly different from that of the class society of old. According to *Low wages and welfare,* in social democratic capitalism, the large majority of well-to-do workers exploited an underclass of a small number of poor, low-income workers and socially excluded individuals hit by economic conditions and shifts in production. *Low wages and welfare* portrayed social services as the affluent society's new poor relief, in which an underclass of outcasts comprised cannon fodder for the production. The position of this new underclass in the margins of society, lacking political resources, made them much more vulnerable than the millions of poor workers who had mobilised to build the people's home. They were a new class of permanently marginalised individuals in the social democratic society, an underclass outside of the working class. The use of the spider web as an illustration in *Low wages and welfare* effectively captured this picture of the individual as locked into social structures and powerless in the web of social exclusion.

Radical social policies

By the early 1970s, the critique that had started in 1967 as investigations of the shortcomings of the people's home had escalated into a scathing repudiation of social democratic policy and its preoccupation with growth. Its conclusion was that neither growth nor modern social policies had reduced class distinctions and insecurity. Economic development did not lead to increased security, the expansion of welfare and an increase in the living standard; it did not create 'strong, competitive consumers', as the Social Policy Committee had intended in the mid-1960s; rather, it created outcasts. The idea of social exclusion as something that would not disappear with economic growth, but as something that was actively created by growth and production led social workers and LO economists to demand a radically different social problem-solving process, one aimed at the social structures that created social exclusion, and that ultimately would concentrate on production conditions and growth.

At their seminars in 1968 and 1969, dominated by heated discussions of the results of the Committee on Low Income, the social workers explicitly discussed the problem of social exclusion as something created by the SAP's slack approach to the needs of production, and by social planning that was far too controlled by the idea of economic growth. The dramatic increases in the demand for social services during the 1960s was related to the growth of social exclusion, following on from a 'sorting out' from production of vulnerable groups and a moralistic and harmful attitude that the socially vulnerable should also participate in production. Activist social policies, rehabilitation and retraining only recreated the problems, since they brought back weak individuals to the production structures that had eliminated them in the first place. The primary objective of social legislation – to return socially problematic groups to production – was a demand with unreasonable and inhuman consequences for individuals who were not socially capable of managing the stresses of modern life.[16]

To the social workers, then, the SAP's social policies were a highly defensive and inefficient system built on values that were far from socialist, subordinated as it was to the needs and growth goals of production and limited to managing the consequences of production. A social policy that contented itself with returning excluded individuals to production and thereby created new social problems represented a deeply conservative force in a class society and could not be regarded as socialist. The FSS demanded a different solution, one that broke with productivism and social policy's growth approach, and gave social policy a more genuinely social content. Efficient social policy problem-solving demanded that social policy concentrate on changing social structures that the FSS believed were creating the problems, instead of 'only' taking care of the already excluded.

> In the prosperous society that has sprung up, social policy and perhaps to a particularly high degree, social services, have become a means for the rationalisation of an economic system whose task – using national production as an indicator – is to increase annual economic growth as much as possible ... In the long run, it is not acceptable for social policy's main objective to be to reduce the injurious effects of the economic system ... This defensive social policy has preserved and, in many cases, magnified the already existing class distinctions and given rise to new disparities among the different groups in society. Therefore, this must be replaced by an offensive social policy, whose most important goal is to work to stop society from evolving into simply a production and consumption apparatus with GDP as its primary valuation instrument. But even this task is too defensive. The new goals for social policy must be designed to have a controlling effect far beyond social policy's borders. It is particularly important that economic policy not be viewed as superior to social policy and that the content of the objectives of social policy be changed to address the growth philosophy that, to a considerable extent, characterises present economic policies.[17]

A radical social policy was a social policy that took priority over economic policy and controlled the organisation of production instead of the reverse. Social policy must be given what the directors of social welfare services and the collaborative committee called a 'structural' role, whereby problem-solving was directed at economic structures and not at individuals. The fundamental objectives of social policy should not be growth, but the creation of individual security.

In 1967 the minister of social affairs, Sven Aspling, appointed a commission whose task was to examine social legislation. The social workers immediately established a shadow commission.[18] They were dissatisfied with the directives to the commission and sceptical of what they believed would be a continuation of traditional social policy instead of the radically new content in social policy that they wanted. They also wanted to ensure that their professional knowledge of social problems and exclusion from the field would be taken into account and laid as the basis of a new social legislation. They demanded that the overarching objective of the social legislation, which had been formulated in the 1950s as the reintegration of individuals into production, be replaced with social objectives, which the social workers formulated as 'security', 'equality' and 'democracy', and that these objectives serve as guiding stars not only for social policy but for all economic and social planning.[19]

The demands of the directors of social welfare services for a radical social policy and social planning characterised by social goals were underscored with the publication of the topical book *Sociala mål i samhällsplaneringen* (*Social goals in social planning*). This pamphlet, also published by a group of LO economists, was a critical commentary of the economic five-year prognosis of 1970. The LO's Economic department had published critical commentaries of the five-year prognoses on several occasions, usually with regard to welfare policy, employment or redistribution, but *Social goals in social planning* was exceptionally critical of the social democratic government and shared many of the points of departure of *Low wages and welfare*. However, whereas *Low wages and welfare* was perhaps too outspokenly critical of 'social democratic capitalism' and only got a very brief mention at the LO congress in 1971, *Social goals in social planning* started a major debate within the LO – a debate that in many ways also pointed forwards to the 1970s ideas on economic democracy and wage-earner funds.

The five-year prognosis of 1970 was extremely troubled by the deterioration in the Swedish balance of payments and wanted to further narrow the growth objective, while tightening consumption in the public sector. Although it was very much aware of the ongoing discussion on low wages and social exclusion as the negative consequence of growth, it brushed aside this discussion by referring to an economic situation in which growth was becoming more and more pressing. It was this affirmation of the principles of post-war economic policy that triggered the LO economists' critique. *Socials goals and social planning* dismissed as preposterous the notion that society would continue to be guided by economic planning that led to wide-scale social exclusion, and insisted that the design of economic planning in the Swedish model should be questioned fundamentally and that economic objectives of growth and productivity be replaced by an overarching political objective of individual security. The book went so far as to call into question growth as the conceptual basis for planning, and called for its replacement with security.[20] In this discussion, the living standard concept acquired additional relevance. The LO book suggested that GDP, as the measure of growth and national income, be replaced with the living standard measure as a much more adequate measure of economic and social progress. It would permit measuring progress in terms of real increased security and well-being, and it would take negative effects of economic growth on the social situation of individuals into account. Living standard components would also make it possible to continually measure welfare changes and thereby arrive at an index for social progress. In its polemic against the five-year prognosis, the group also stated that the living standard concept could be used to measure the efficiency of welfare production. According to the group, the living standard concept ought to facilitate social productivity measurements of production within the public sector. This concept was better suited for discussing productivity within social policy than were economic indices. The social effects of social policy, not the economic value of production, were important. The living standard concept was also a way of arriving at better productivity gauges for the public sector's production – the latter could not be quantified in the GNP because it was set at zero, a problem in Swedish planning since the concept of GDP had been introduced in the 1950s.[21]

The social cost of growth

This 1960s critique set in place an economic discourse around the problem of social exclusion in economic terms. Social exclusion was defined as the social cost for economic expansion, the price to pay for economic growth, in the form of the exhaustion and waste of social capital. The idea of human exhaustion and waste was put forward in *Low wages and welfare,* which claimed that the welfare losses created by post-war rationalisation policies must be included in the economic assessment of productivity gains.[22] Per Holmberg, the secretary of the Committee on Low Income, also defined social exclusion as the social cost of growth at a seminar of the social workers, held in Ronneby in 1971. Holmberg pointed to the economic contradiction in a situation where production trends that created exclusion and led to increased costs for social reform were considered as productive in any way:

> In actual fact, this exhaustion and exclusion of individuals in industrial life will continue to represent an economic paradox as long as the national product is calculated as it is. If companies generate extra profits, this often has to do with the fact that exhaustion and the exclusion of labour have been particularly widespread. In that case, social policy ... has been affected by a steadily increasing commitment and expenditures that are also included in national production. But actually, a large share of these socio-political expenses should be considered as negative entries in the national product – in the same way that one now wants different types of pollution to be considered negatively. Grotesque as it may seem, in terms of current calculations, the greater the national product's inflation, the greater the social expenditures.[23]

In this discussion, Holmberg dismissed the SAP's historical definition of social policy as a productive investment as misconstrued. Just as it was contradictory to regard productivity gains that caused social problems as productive, it was contradictory to view social policy's expansion as a part of a productive expansion when instead, it should be regarded as a negative entry, as a cost for taking care of worn-out individuals. In Holmberg's interpretation, social policy could not be considered productive, as it did not free up human resources; rather, it attended to the costs of production in the form of human waste. Social policy was not an investment in economic efficiency, but the cost for inefficiency.

Reaction and rejection

In the critique from the directors of social welfare services and the LO economists, an interpretative framing in which growth was seen as the creator of insecurity and social problems was established – a framing that was in stark contrast to that of the strong society. This critique became a sensitive subject for social democracy. In the midst of its belief that the good society had finally been created, these pictures of systematic exclusion came to the fore. The critique's framing of 'social exclusion' as something that had been created by a social democratic policy for security and its depiction of the strong society's social policies as re-created poor relief had great symbolic significance.

Social democracy's initial reaction in the late 1960s was to reject the critique's image of reality. It was not consistent with the strong society's worldview of steadily growing security in the affluent society and its understanding of social problems as being rooted in historic production conditions. It was, quite simply, a reality that was completely unthinkable from within the ideology of the strong society.

During a historic radio debate, the Minister of Finance Gunnar Sträng greeted Per Holmberg with this question: 'What person, sound of body and mind, would work for less than five kronor an hour?'[24] The implication was clear: in a social democratic society of full employment and solidary wage bargaining, only those in some way handicapped could possibly remain poor. In 1971, the Committee on Low Income was disbanded by the Prime Minister and party leader Olof Palme. Palme's act was widely perceived as a way of quickly silencing criticism that had become increasingly difficult to refute and that pointed to the failure of the SAP to create security for all. Later, in a 1977 book on current affairs, Olof Palme commented on the termination with the argument that the Committee had produced enough statistics:

> I wish to categorically deny that the Committee on Low Income was, in this case, cut off. This is the way it was portrayed, but we were able to verify that all the fundamental empirical evidence we needed had already been produced and published. At that level, there were no more reports to be written. Now it was time to take action.[25]

After the Committee was disbanded, a group was appointed to 'evaluate' its work.[26] To pacify the Committee's articulate secretary and cries of outrage in the public debate, Per Holmberg, the Committee's secretary, was also asked to write a report but when this recommended that the living standard measure be developed into a theoretical concept that dealt with issues of citizenship, empowerment and individual freedom, it was rapidly buried.[27] The evaluation group carried out an extensive analysis of the Committee on Low Income's statistical work but was unable to find any errors. However, it did its best to dismiss its findings. The group's final report observed that the Committee on Low Income could be considered as '*one* researcher's recommendations', that its conclusions were 'contributions to a debate' that contained 'very little that was new' and that it was 'difficult to believe that consensus would ever prevail regarding these issues'.[28] Further, the Committee had lent itself to a series of 'rash interpretations' regarding the failure of social democratic policy.[29] Accordingly, the reaction to the Committee's findings and the criticism to which they gave rise was to reject these findings and, in this way, attempt to exclude its picture of reality.

We can afford to be generous to the weak in our society

The first reaction of the SAP to the critique of the late 1960s, therefore, was to try to silence it. But behind these defensive reactions, a gradual process of ideological rearticulation began, one that tried instead to face up to these images of a radically changed social reality and incorporate it into social democratic ideology. In 1967, an extra party congress was summoned partly in reaction to the debate surrounding the findings of the Committee on Low Income, and partly in reaction to the early signs of problems for the Swedish export industry, with rising prices on international markets. In an emotionally charged speech, LO Chairman Arne Geijer took up the matters of unfinished welfare, the working environment and social exclusion.[30] Geijer's contribution led to the appointment of the Equality Group, under the leadership of Alva Myrdal, then Minister of Disarmament.[31]

The purpose of the Equality Group was to focus on the security and equality aspects of economic and social change, and bring these aspects to the fore.[32] Its appointment implied a certain recognition of the possibility that the party had, in the post-war period, perhaps been too preoccupied with economic issues and had let go of the question of equality. Clearly, the Equality Group was also appointed to create a response to the critique from the left and rethink the concept of equality in the light of the problem of social exclusion, and subsequently it was also charged with the problem of how to deal ideologically with the possibility that the new social problems were effects of the very policies put in place to bring about the people's home. When Alva Myrdal presented the guiding principles for the Group's work at the regular party congress in 1968, she made it clear that what had emerged as a radically different social reality made great demands on social democracy and that it could not simply be dismissed as mere statistics or misguided conclusions:

> Indeed, today's situation is not a satisfactory one for everyone, even in our rich country . . . a lot of new material that is critical of society – for example, *Unfinished welfare* by the Inghes – has uncovered severe deficiencies.[33]

However, the group's report, *More equality*, published in 1969, was a strained document. It was inherently cautious. It was acutely aware of the SAP's increasingly vulnerable position and it refused to speak explicitly of social exclusion as a consequence of post-war social democratic policy. It walked a delicate tightrope between, on the one hand, talking about the new problems and on the other, avoiding all discussion of 'consequences'. Instead, it spoke loosely of 'change itself'. It was the general process of change that had created exclusion, not social democracy. [34]

Still, this outlook of the Equality Report on the process of change stands in marked contrast to the strong society's notion of progress and its optimistic ideas of social and economic development as processes that go hand-in-hand. In the report of the Equality Group, change was depicted as deeply disconcerting and worrying. In a situation where new social problems could apparently come about as a result of the very policies meant to eradicate them, the process of change seemed fundamentally unpredictable. Development was not a friction-free process of gradual evolution towards the completion of the people's home.

In the 1969 report, the post-war social democratic world of ideas was described as an illusion, characterised by a misguided and naïve belief in progress. Need and insecurity were not the remains of older conditions and former stages of capitalism; rather, they were constantly reshaped under changing economic and social conditions. Thus, the problem was twofold: not only had social democracy not succeeded in overcoming old inequalities, rooted in the old society, but furthermore, new inequalities had arisen as vulnerable groups had been passed over in the evolution of living standards and left behind by production changes. Perhaps the most striking difference between the world-view of the Equality Report and that of the strong society was the conception that there were groups that could not manage the speed of the structural transformation: groups that, for a variety of reasons, were handicapped by modern society, with its fast-paced production and working life.[35] Not everyone was alike, not everyone could partake in change on the same terms. This development made great demands on social democracy and its solidarity with 'the very weakest':

> ... we [must not] cast aside the very weakest, who are weak primarily as a result of the achievement- and competitive mentality that still dominates many aspects of society – this in spite of the inroads that social democratic policy has made with respect to many issues. We can afford to be generous toward those who have not succeeded in our complicated society.[36]

'We can afford to be generous' was a very different conception of solidarity than the emphasis on productive participation as the basis for inclusion in the strong society. Here, the idea that there was a group that was weak, that was not productive, and that called for solidarity and 'generosity' was accepted.

The limit of the Equality Report was its refusal to speak explicitly of new social inequalities as consequences of previous party policies, and to this extent, its failure to also provide an articulate analysis of the problem of social exclusion. Between the lines, however, the report contained a clear rejection of the Rehn-Meidner model and of the productivism of the post-war period. There were also embryos of suggestions that broke new ideological ground for the SAP, as the report made vague suggestions of reforms such as a citizen's wage, as a social policy reform that would strengthen individual rights and avoid a direct link between social policy and productive participation. The report also contained a critique of universalism and the underlying ideas in the notion of 'general social policies' that had been a core postulate of party ideology since it was introduced during the Depression by the legendary minister of social affairs Gustav Möller. To treat everybody equally, the Equality Report stated, was not enough. Equal treatment was a liberal conception that failed to recognise that individuals had different starting points in life. To break the vicious circles that trapped individuals in social exclusion and marginalisation, social democracy must accept a concept of equality that went further and that compensated the weak for their weaknesses. This was the meaning of a generous attitude.

Thus, in the work of the Equality Group, there emerged the beginnings of an ideological reformulation and an embracing of the new reality, that, cautious as it was, broke with the ideas of the strong society. This was a deeply contradictory process as the Equality Group, on the one hand, called for a radicalised concept of equality and argued that the SAP had in fact not done enough to protect the individual from the effects of change, and on the other, seemed to accept that not everyone could keep up and that some would inevitably fall behind.

In defence of growth

The suggestions of the Equality Group, in spite of the cautious formulations that surrounded them, were far from party orthodoxy and stirred up bad blood. In a letter to Alva Myrdal, Gösta Rehn called the Equality Report a 'wish list', and wondered why it was necessary to 'condemn as asocial' the entire post-war economic policy.[37]

> I know that Rudolf [Meidner] has a guilty conscience for this, but if one looks at the relevant writings, one will find that the LO economists can have a very clear conscience on this point ... the same applies to the Labour Market Report [*Arbetsmarknadsutredningen 1965:9*] and the proposition subsequently built on it, in which one paragraph after another stresses the importance of combining the economic aspects with or subordinating them to the social ones, namely, human considerations. We were very much aware that we did not wish to accept the frequently recurring approach that 'one must mobilize marginalised labour reserves in order to take care of labour shortages'. Active labour market policies would, of course, serve the people, not the reverse! ... We ... have sought ways to make economic and social goals correspond with one other; surely, there is nothing wrong with that, since both sets of goals benefit.[38]

To Rehn, the danger of the Equality Report was that it departed from the careful consideration of the balance between economic and social objectives in post-war party thinking, separated them as if they were antagonistic, and made suggestions on social reforms without considering their economic impact.[39]

Rehn was not the only one to find the report Utopian, and the policy suggestions of the report, vague as they were, were not picked up upon by the party leadership.

But the fundamental concern with the balance between economic and social development that the Equality Report so clearly expressed mirrored party discourse. The 1967 congress, at which the Equality Group was appointed, also approved new economic guidelines under the slogan 'Work, Security, Progress'. In the guidelines, the objectives of the economic policy were broadened to also include responsibility for 'security in development' and, through comprehensive planning, for 'preventing disastrous social consequences'.[40] Security was a new concept in the explicit motivations of economic policy. However, just as the Equality Group could not bring itself to address social exclusion as a consequence of growth policies, there was a fundamental limit to the debate on economic policy, and that was the stand on the concept of growth. The party executive's declaration on economic policy clearly stressed growth as the basis for continued security development:

> Only a society with expanding resources had the prerequisites to solve basic economic and social problems.[41]

Economic policy, therefore, emphasised growth, in accordance with the strong society's framings. According to the economic discussion, growth was even more vital in the current situation for spreading security and a decent living standard to those groups that had not yet had their share. In this way, the interpretation of the problem of social exclusion in the party's economic policy discourse in the late 1960s was to strengthen the priority of growth, albeit with an added emphasis on redistribution. In 1968, the party's economic policy report recommended an active economic policy that would take greater responsibility for the creation of growth and its diffusion to marginalised groups.[42]

This defence of the concept of growth did not go silently by at the party congress, where Per Holmberg, perhaps predictably, argued that continued growth carried with it the risk of bringing about still more social exclusion. Holmberg's objection was refuted by Minister of Finance Gunnar Sträng, who further underscored the importance of the Labour movement's support of growth, particularly in a time of increasing economic uncertainty.[43]

Consequently, the SAP's reaction to the critique in the late 1960s was primarily to defend the ideological postulates of the strong society, and growth as the ideological priority. The idea of a negative relationship between growth and security, in which growth created social problems and insecurity, was a difficult one for the SAP. The Party's defensive reactions can be viewed as an attempt to defend the ideology of the strong society and keep growth and security together as concordant goals. Social democracy's reaction to the debate on social exclusion and the critique of growth was to insist that security required growth. Accordingly, its dominant interpretation of the problem of social exclusion was that the creation of more security required more growth, while the notion that growth might actually create insecurity was excluded from the party debate.

This fundamental limit to how the party dealt with the critique of growth became clear in the party leader Olof Palme's rhetoric. Olof Palme had a double-edged attitude to the younger generation and the late 1960s critique of social democracy. On the one hand, Palme was a young leader, one who embraced the values of the new generation in terms of gender equality, solidarity with the Third World, and a perhaps more individualistic approach to social democratic ideology. Palme, as Minister of Education, was the one to face the students that had occupied parts of the buildings of Stockholm University in 1968 and he famously ended up debating their demands for reform with them. Palme was also the Western leader who took perhaps the strongest stand against the Vietnam war when he marched through Stockholm side by side with the North Vietnamese ambassador in a demonstration against the bombings of Hanoi, causing a standstill in Swedish–American relations.[44] But on the other hand, Palme was, in the interior domestic debate, fiercely anti-communist and very cautious of the influence of Marxism on the younger generation. Palme attended one of the social workers' seminars in 1971, at which the social workers vigorously attacked social democracy as a pro-capitalist movement and the centrality of the growth concept in social democratic ideology. The idea of the strong society was especially targeted as something that had come to encompass a harsh and brutal social reality:

> We believe that a strong society is needed to exterminate the tough society, and we hope that our ideas will have enough of an impact to make more and more people understand that the strong society will not be the protector of a tough society![45]

Palme beat back the criticism with a speech that eloquently made the ideological case for growth. He sternly defended the idea that growth and security were intrinsically linked, and that this was a necessary postulate of social reformism. He cautioned the social workers against attacking that which was actually the prerequisite for social policy and social security, namely, growth. In Palme's view, the 1970s would see even greater increases in production. If the price for this was more social exclusion, then the price was too high. But if increases in production meant that people's difficulties could be levelled out, 'well, then it is worth the price'.[46]

Palme went on to explain the relationship between economic and social policy to the mutinous social workers. According to Palme, there was a close relationship between social policy and economic policy. Growth created the conditions for social policy and social policy created growth. Social policy was a prerequisite for an efficient society, and social policy and economic policy enjoyed a common goal in society's development. To separate them was, in Palme's view, a crucial mistake:

> [social policy and economic policy] must be different sides of a total policy and thus, intimately dependent on and contingent upon one another. This is not a question of some one-sided dependence. There are those who are trying to depict the expenditures for labour market policy or social policy as burdens. Sometimes, they believe that these burdens must be borne so that the productive economic policy can be taken

> further. It appears that this notion of a requisite antagonism between economic policy and the social goals for societal development is shared with those who criticise growth. In my opinion, the investments in labour market and social policies are productive in the truly fundamental sense of the word. We can demonstrate that the social reform legislation did not constitute a burden for the economy; rather it was primarily a stimulus, a driving force for the economic growth of the country. Why am I arguing so strongly? Well, because if one maintains that it is difficult to pursue social policy during rapid economic growth, I would like to argue that if we are striving for rapid economic growth, then we must pursue an effective social policy. The explanation is simple. In this way, we liberate people so that they can work together in this country; then, with increased economic growth, we will become a more productive society. If we wish to go forward, we must seek out innovations, in not only new technology and inventions; it is at least as important that we also pursue the demands for renewal in the social sector.[47]

Palme expressly warned the social workers, a professional group that had traditionally sided with the party, against setting the economic and social goals in opposition to one another and falling for a romantic flirtation with revolutionary Marxism. To Palme, to bring out a conflict between social and economic policy, between the ideological objectives of security and growth, would be to open the door to an age-old criticism from the right that viewed social policy as an expenditure and burden for growth. Social policy, to Palme, was productive, 'in the truly fundamental sense of the word':[48]

> The purpose of these simple arguments about growth is to establish the following: economic growth and social policy must not be viewed as enemies. Instead, I believe that social policy stimulates growth. At the same time, growth is a prerequisite for the solidarity that supports socio-political efforts. *Security and growth go hand-in-hand.* [Emphasis added][49]

He finished his speech with the warning, aimed at the more radical elements among the social workers, that overthrowing the capitalist system was not a good method of social work. Social problems would not go away with revolutionary upheaval; they would return as 'phoenixes from the ashes'. Also after the revolution, people would need the help of social workers.[50]

Concluding remarks

The late 1960s critique targeted what was both the strength and the Achilles heel of the SAP; its fundamental growth orientation. The strong society's optimistic idea of development was turned on its head – growth did not create security but insecurity, alienation and social exclusion. Post-war social democracy's dream of the productive society was dismissed as a quantitative and technocratic illusion that reproduced capitalist structures and led to fundamental inefficiencies and human waste, all in the name of social democracy. In its most radical form, the critique escalated to calling into question the very notion of growth and the fundamental subordination of social policy to economic policy in the capitalist economy.

This debate came as a shock to the SAP. Its first, defensive reactions to the Committee on Low Income and its discomfort with the work of the Equality Group is indicative of the extent to which the idea of social exclusion was simply unthinkable from within the worldview of the strong society. It was an image of reality that was directly in confrontation with ideology. It seemed to target the heart of social democratic ideology, the idea that economic dynamism could be coupled with a public responsibility for the protection of all. The idea that the SAP had allowed the process of change to vent itself upon society's weak was difficult to take in. Moreover this debate was strategically problematic. Palme's assertion to the social workers in 1971 – 'security and growth go hand-in-hand as friends' – made it clear that he was acutely aware of the importance of continuing to assert social policy's role in growth for the purpose of defending further social reforms. The SAP's defensive reactions departed in this historic understanding. However, behind the SAP's defensive reactions and initial attempts to hold on to the articulations of the strong society, a gradual process of rearticulation had begun. Perhaps the most important aspect of this was the replacement of the strong society's assertive outlook on change as a virtuous spiral of economic and social progress with a growing fear that social democracy had not been able to control capitalism to the extent believed, and a shocked realisation that new problems of inequality and insecurity had arisen as consequences of reformism itself.

Notes

1 Inghe, G. and Inghe, M., 1967, *Den ofärdiga välfärden*, Tiden, Stockholm; Inghe, G., 1960, *Fattiga i folkhemmet*, Tiden, Stockholm, p. 4.
2 SOU 1967:36.
3 Fridjonsdottir, K., 1991, 'Social science and the Swedish model. Sociology at the service of the welfare state', in Wagner, P., Wittrock, B. and Whitley, R. (eds), *Discourses on society. The shaping of the social science disciplines*, Kluwer, Dortrecht; Therborn 1983; Heclo 1987; Lundberg, U. and Åmark, K., 1997, 'En vänster i takt med tiden? 1960–talets politiska kultur i 90–talets självförståelse', *Häften för kritiska studier*, 2, 1997, Stockholm.
4 See Wagner, P., 2001, *A history and theory of the social sciences – not all that is solid melts into air*, Sage, New York; Wagner, P., 1991, *Sozialwissenschaften und staat, Frankreich, Italien, Deutschland 1970–1980*, Campus Verlag, Frankfurt.
5 FSS 1966, *Serviceinriktad socialvård*; 1967, *Sociallagstiftningen, hjälpmedel eller hinder*; 1968, *Socialvården söker nya vägar*; 1970, *Alternativ socialvård*; 1971, *Socialvård i framtiden*; 1972, *Ekonomi och välfärd.*
6 SOU 1970:34 p. 10.
7 SSU 1967, *Inkomstklyftor och standardhöjning*, Stockholm; Holmberg, P., 1970, *Välstånd med slagsida*, Publica, Stockholm; LO 1971, *Låglön och välfärd, rapport till LO:s lönepolitiska kommitté.*
8 Ingmar Svennilson was replaced by Rudolf Meidner in 1967.
9 I am grateful to Rudolf Meidner for discussing this with me.
10 Sundbom, L., 1970, *De extremt lågavlönade*, pp. 12–24, 62–63; SOU 1970:34 pp. 17–24; SOU 1971:39; SOU 1972:44 pp. 16–17.

11 Katz, M.B., 1989, *The undeserving poor. From president Johnson's war on poverty to President Reagan's war on welfare*, Pantheon books, New York; O'Connor, A., 2001, *Poverty knowledge: social science, social policy, and the poor in 20th century US history*, Princeton University Press, Princeton.
12 This discussion was influenced by Titmuss's ideas of social citizenship: see Titmuss R., 1958, *Essays on the welfare state*, Allen and Unwin, London.
13 Johansson, S., 1970, *Om levnadsnivåundersökningen*, pp. 5–12, 19–25.
14 LO 1971.
15 LO 1971 pp. 104, 106, 108, 120.
16 FSS 1970 pp. 7–14, 154.
17 FSS 1971 pp. 17.
18 SOU 1974:39 p. 21f. FSS 1970 p. 10; FSS 1971 p. 14.
19 FSS archives, volume F2, 3.
20 Burstedt, Å. (ed), 1971, *Sociala mål i samhällsplaneringen*, Tiden, Stockholm, pp. 9, 84.
21 Burstedt 1971 pp. 86, 106.
22 LO 1971 p. 132.
23 FSS 1972 p. 58. Cf. LO 1971 p. 174.
24 '*Det begriper du väl att ingen riktigt funtad å kroppens och huvudets vägnar skulle jobba för under 5 kronor i timmen ...*', quoted from Elmbrandt 1989 p. 109.
25 Palme, O., 1977, *Med egna ord, Samtal med Serge Richard och Nordal Åkerman*, Tiden, Stockholm, p. 65. Sadly, very little of Palme's writing has been translated into English.
26 Ds In 1972:19.
27 Ds In 1971:16; Johansson, S., 1979, *Mot en teori för social rapportering*, Stockholm, Institute for Social Research (SOFI).
28 Ds In 1972:19 s. 14f. My italics.
29 Ds In 1972:19 p. 38.
30 SAP 1967 conference protocol pp. 356–363.
31 Alva Myrdal was, with her husband Gunnar, a radical thinker on social policy in the 1930s, a proponent of women's rights in the 1940s and 1950s, head of Unesco's department of social science 1951–55 and Swedish ambassador to India. She was awarded the Nobel Peace prize in 1982. See Bok, S., 1991, *Alva Myrdal. A daughter's memoir*, Addison-Wesley, Reading, MA.
32 The Equality Group consisted of Alva Myrdal, Lars Ahlvarsson, Annika Baude, Torsten Eliasson, Valdemar Lundberg, Lisa Mattson, Arne Pettersson, Mats Hellström, Villy Bergström, Lars Hallsten, Enn Kokk, Ingela Thalén and Nordal Åkerman.
33 SAP 1968 conference protocol p. 190.
34 SAP 1969, *Ökad jämlikhet*, p. 15. See Tilton 1990 p. 218f.
35 SAP 1969 pp. 10–15.
36 SAP 1969 p. 112f.
37 Letter from Gösta Rehn to Alva Myrdal May 4 1969, Alva Myrdal's archives, volume 64 c. 1.
38 Ibid.
39 It seems that the two architects of the Rehn-Meidner model, Gösta Rehn and Rudolf Meidner, interpreted the problems of low wages and social exclusion very differently. Rehn was obviously outraged at the suggestions that active labour market policies were to blame for problems of social exclusion or human exhaustion. Meidner,

however, was chair of the Committee on Low Income, and even if he did not actively take part in the Committee's work, he did not try to disassociate himself from it. Meidner went on, in the 1970s, to devise his suggestions for wage earner funds that were an attempt to increase wage earners' control over production and a cornerstone of the 1970s strategy for economic democracy.

40 SAP 1968 p. 9. See Benner 1997 p. 109f.
41 SAP 1967 conference protocol p. 186.
42 SAP 1968 pp. 6, 10.
43 SAP 1968 conference protocol p. 61.
44 See Östberg 2002.
45 FSS 1970 p. 22.
46 FSS 1970 p. 193.
47 FSS 1972 p. 189.
48 FSS 1972 p. 189.
49 FSS 1972 p. 189. The Swedish quote is '*man ska mäla dem samman som vänner*'.
50 Ibid.

4

Social policy for security

Introduction

The late 1960s signified a break with the post-war optimism regarding growth. The post-war view of growth as a promise for social development was replaced by understandings of growth as a threat to social progress, and as a source of new problems in a changing, uncertain period of societal development.

Politics in the 1960s and 1970s were marked by the discovery of the outermost limits to growth. In the debate on the environment, as well as in discussions on the social consequences of growth, it was pointed out that post-war economic expansion had led to the exhaustion of production factors such as natural resources or social capital. In politics, these experiences led to dystopic interpretations of the growth society's unsustainability and capitalism's inherent destructiveness, but also to attempts reshape politics in order to refute and control this problematic side of growth.[1] The 1970s were therefore characterised by a fundamental shift from the post-war focus on economic expansion, to a focus on sustainable development. This meant a change in the meaning and standing of the concept of growth in politics. In international economic planning, experiments were made with alternative measurements of progress, that took into account the spillover effects and negative externalities of production on society. Environmental problems were clothed in economic terms and discussed as negative entries that should be taken into account in assessments of growth. In the social planning of the early 1970s, a parallel discussion on how to assess and measure the social costs of growth and find a basis for socially sustainable capitalism began.[2]

The ideological changes within the SAP in the 1970s must be viewed in light of this generally altered understanding of growth. In the 1970s, the so far hegemonic standing of the concept of growth in the Swedish Labour movement was challenged by a number of alternative goal formulations. Problems of economic and social development in sparsely populated areas in the Swedish north led to the formulation of a social democratic regional policy, in which the need to preserve the countryside was posited against the need for growth.[3] The SAP was faced with heated opposition from environmental groups over the exploitation of Swedish rivers for energy purposes, and the so-called 'battle of the elm trees' in the Stockholm park Kungsträdgården in 1972 has become a landmark in Swedish political history. The publication of Ralf Edberg's *Skuggan av ett moln* (*The shadow of a cloud*) became to the Swedish debate what Rachel Carson's *Silent spring* was in the US, and it triggered a discussion within the Labour movement on the conflict between growth and intangible resources such as clean air and water.[4] The growing discussion on economic democracy, the work environment, and eventually the wage-earner funds debate contained a similar juxtaposition of growth and intangible values, where the security and participation of workers were posited against production profits and rationalisation.[5] The economic programme that was launched at the 1967 congress, in which the objectives of economic policy were expanded to include the creation of 'security in development', continued.

The developments in the SAP in the 1970s have been described as an 'offensive' in economic policy, whereby social democracy increased the scope of economic planning and went further into the production sphere in order to strengthen control over long term developments.[6] In the social sphere, the 1970s saw a radicalisation of the party's standing in social and welfare issues, in what has been described as an 'equality wave' within the Labour movement. The public sector expanded vigorously in the 1970s in an attempt to meet increased demands for equality within a number of areas, especially in the 1975 promises for daycare expansion that followed the Party's embracing of the principle of gender equality.[7]

Consequently, the ideological changes of the 1970s saw a radicalisation of social democracy's positions on production, and a greater ideological emphasis both on the control of the organisation of production and on the distribution of its results.

This chapter discusses the changes in the 1970s as the gradual emergence of a new ideology in reaction to the critique of the late 1960s. This can be discussed in terms of an ideological crisis of social democracy. This crisis was directly related to the changed standing of the concept of growth in social democratic ideology. The rearticulation of growth from a solution to social problems to being the problem itself created profound tensions in the strong society's worldview. The previous chapter discussed social democracy's initial reaction to the critique of the late 1960s, which was to retain and defend the strong society's framings and particularly the standing of growth in party ideology. But in the transition between the 1960s and 1970s, a gradual process began where the SAP's defensive position and ambivalent reactions to the critique were replaced by ideological rearticulation and eventually with a break with the strong society's framings. In this process, the SAP incorporated the metaphors and definitions of the problem of social exclusion that had been put forward in critique of party ideology in the late 1960s.

Social democracy and the price of growth

In the early 1970s, social democracy gradually formulated a theory of social exclusion as a problem intrinsically related to industrial capitalism. Whereas the Equality Group discussed the problem of social exclusion in terms of the unpredictability and changeability of social development but would not speak of a direct relationship between growth and insecurity, in the SAP's programmes and conference debates of the 1970s, social exclusion was now framed as a consequence of post-war economic policies. Problems of marginalisation in sparsely populated regions, and segregation, alienation, and crime in the suburban areas (and particularly in the council estates of the *miljonprogrammet*[8] that had come about as part of the SAP's strategy for urbanisation), were now addressed explicitly as the consequences of growth.[9] With metaphors such as 'exhaustion', 'price' and 'expenditure', an interpretation of social exclusion as the economic cost for growth was also established within social democracy.

Following from this interpretation of social exclusion, the party also gradually began to rethink the concept of growth. Olof Palme's rhetoric underwent a significant change from his defensive reactions in the public debate and his aggressive attacks on the revolutionary tendencies of young social workers to expressions of deep concern. In the early 1970s, Palme returned again and again to the problem of growth – the hope of the previous generation of social democracy, now the origin of social conflict, ideological polarisation and human suffering. In his writings and speeches he incorporated the critique's definition of social exclusion as the social costs for growth; the social 'price' to pay for the gains of the post-war production.

In a 1971 economic commentary Palme wrote that growth had 'social limits'. Growth was no longer created the way it had been in the post-war period – by putting idle production factors to work and activating labour market reserves. Growth now seemed to be created through the systematic exhaustion of human resources. From this perspective, Palme added, it was not so strange that Swedish social workers attacked growth 'because that is how they really see the problem in the reality they are in'.[10]

Palme now saw a deep antagonism between growth's promises of material prosperity and the threat that growth posed to social progress:

> Growth has social limits. It is no longer created by putting social resources and labour reserves to work ... It is created through the destruction of social resources. It is not strange from this perspective that our social workers attack growth. This is how they see the problems in the reality they work in ... What has happened during 30 years in which we believed in the harmony between growth and social development, is that the price for growth, from a social point of view, has become much higher. A tension has arisen between a growth ethic that is deeply rooted in our culture and the fear of its social consequences.[11]

In the early 1970s, Palme returned to this antagonism in a series of declarations. He obviously perceived the issue of growth as a fundamental problem for social democracy, a social movement that had gone so far in the postwar period to defend the ideological value of growth. In a 1972 commentary to the Club of Rome's recently published *The limits to growth,* Palme wrote that the critique of growth called into question the industrial society's basic values. In doing so, it had created a deep polarisation between those groups in society who wanted to defend growth at any price and those that were now arguing for a limited growth rate or even for no growth at all.[12]

In his correspondence with West Germany's leader Willy Brandt and Austria's Chancellor Bruno Kreisky on the situation on social democracy in the early 1970s, Palme likened the political situation of the 1970s to that of the 1930s, with growing revolutionary and totalitarian currents in society, growing social protests, and increased polarisation between left and right understandings of the economy. Particularly, he referred to the problem of growth as social democracy's big dilemma for the 1970s. The demands facing social democracy in the 1970s were for 'good things', for social democratic values such as security and equality, but the crux, to Palme, was that protecting these values seemed to require both more of that which was accused of being at the root of all social evils, growth, and, at the same time, less of it. Palme was also troubled by the possibility that the growth critique ran the risk of uniting the critics of social democracy from both the left and the right. In their critique of social democracy's growth concept, the opponents of growth shared common ground with those who criticised social democracy's interference in free market capitalism.[13] In Palme's opinion, social democracy's future depended on whether or not it could successfully fulfil these demands.[14] Nevertheless, there was an obvious limit for Palme. Social democracy could not renounce growth as the material basis for reform politics. Social democracy could not permit the discussion on the consequences of growth to escalate into an attack on growth itself.

In one of the somersaults characteristic of Palme's rhetorical skill, he immediately moved on to redefine this 'dilemma' as 'opportunity'. In this growing breach between left and right, and between the 'failed' systems of Soviet communism and American capitalism, both 'obsessed with the myth of growth', Palme now saw an ideological opening for a new middle or third way for social democracy and its classic emphasis on controlled and regulated capitalism. This third way required that social democracy break with the post-war idea of growth as unlimited expansion and find new articulations for the role of growth in the modern society; articulations that incorporated the critique from the left and accommodated the demands of a young and post-material generation.

> Ideologically, this situation represents an extraordinary opportunity for democratic socialism. We have never considered growth as an automatic gauge of welfare. For us, the social needs of human beings have been most important – the demand for employment, security and welfare.[15]

The 1970s challenge to social democracy, then, was to find a definition of growth that gave it a social face and could create a genuinely 'social' policy for the 1970s; a new articulation that defended growth as an ideological objective, but strengthened its social side.[16] Therefore, social democracy had to rearticulate growth as a positive social force, and recreate a consensus around growth as something that led to security for individuals. Social democracy had to find a new ideological formulation for the relationship between growth and social security, one that was capable of repudiating rival framings from both right and left, while not letting the actual problems of falling growth rates out of its sight. For Palme, the solution resided in raising expectations on the social plane. Growth's social price required a strengthened social reform policy in the 1970s, one that would succeed in giving growth a social content.[17]

Palme seems to have been rather revived by this whole debate. In a 1974 interview in the daily newspaper *Aftonbladet,* Palme told the political journalist Nordal Åkerman that he had not 'felt so ideologically energised since the 1950s, when we were working with the public sector'. 'The industrial society's hangover' had given rise to an ideological debate on the havoc wreaked by industrial capitalism on human beings and the environment that presented social democracy with the opportunity to finally overcome the 'technocratic growth philosophy of capitalism and communism'.[18]

Welfare and efficiency

So the SAP embarked on a fundamental rethinking of the concept of growth. The question of how to give growth a social content became a core issue in 1970s social democratic ideology. The party conference in 1972 launched such an attempt to reformulate policy, strengthen the interaction between economic and social objectives, and find new articulations of the relationship between growth and security. A considerable portion of the 1972 conference concerned the working environment and economic democracy, questions that went on in party debate throughout the 1970s and culminated in the wage-earner funds proposal in 1978. In his opening speech, Palme summarised the party's work since the 1967 party conference. In working groups and deliberations, the party had responded to the picture of insecurity. The big insight to social democracy in these years was that production profits did not automatically lead to profits for society as a whole. An increase in production 'at the cost of human exhaustion' could not be looked upon as an increase in prosperity. Therefore, the Labour movement must go further in its understanding of growth, formulate growth's social substance and steer growth towards social goals. This required an intensification of economic planning and stronger control and planning of growth and the organisation of production.[19] The party conference was dominated by this discussion on strengthened economic and social planning.

In this debate, the concept of welfare emerged as a new and central element in social democratic ideology. The concept was introduced in the title of the Equality Group's second report, *Välfärd och arbete åt alla* (*Welfare and work for all*), devoted to the concept of welfare (*välfärd*):

> It is obvious that economic growth cannot be used as a comprehensive gauge for measuring society's progress ... The concept of welfare has been given a richer

> content ... Economic growth has been and continues to be necessary in order to eliminate need and shortages and to create the resources that make it possible for human beings to have a better life. However, the Labour movement's assessment of economic growth also requires an assessment of the substance of growth. Economic growth is only useful when it really enriches people's lives. Included in this is the fact that the costs for growth, which perhaps cannot be calculated in economic terms, must be counted in, and above all else, they must not affect vulnerable groups.[20]

Consequently, welfare dealt with an overall perspective on efficiency, where the effects of growth on individual security were taken into account, and where the interplay between economic and social development came to the fore.

The Equality Group's discussion on welfare was very noticeably influenced by the work of the Committee on Low Income's, and the living standard concept as a much wider notion of security that than which had informed party thinking in the post-war period. According to the group, the Labour movement's understanding of social security had changed. Although fewer people were living under difficult economic conditions or were in need, many of them still experienced insecurity in their working life and the social environment. Welfare dealt with all those risks that individuals, including those in socially vulnerable and weak groups, experienced in modern society, as well as with political resources, and the right to take part in the decision-making process and participate in society and working life on equal terms. Since these welfare factors must be included in an assessment of growth, this also meant that the social costs created by production and growth in the form of the consequences of growth on vulnerable groups must also be taken into account.[21]

In order to strengthen the interplay between economic objectives and objectives of security, the party executive had asked the Economic Policy Committee to deliberate with the Equality Group. The report that the Economic Policy Committee submitted to the conference included a programme for intensified economic planning, a 'coordinated economic policy for the 1970s'. This programme had evolved from the 1960s guidelines for an 'active economic policy', the purpose of which had been to strengthen the growth orientation of the Labour movement's economic policies. The wording, 'active economic policy', alluded to the central economic text of the post-war period, namely, the LO's *Coordinated economic policy*, that laid the foundations for the Rehn-Meidner model in the early 1960s.

The report included a lengthy discussion on the objectives of economic policy, in which every effort was made to dissociate the programme from post-war economic policy. It was 'natural', said the report, for 'an increase in production' to have been at the centre of party policy as long as the most basic needs remained. However, in the early 1970s, most basic needs were fulfilled, and people worried about more sophisticated things and values that went beyond material satisfaction, the environment, stress, and feelings of alienation. People wanted 'welfare', and 'quality of life'.[22] These were new concepts in social democratic ideology, and they challenged the role of economic policy and its purpose to bring about social progress. The programme went on from the formulation of the goals of economic policy in the late 1960s as security in development, to formulating the goal of economic policy as 'economic development leading to welfare – not to social exclusion'.[23] In this manner, welfare was explicitly contrasted to social exclusion. According to the report, the objective of welfare meant that production profits needed to be evaluated to determine whether they were fulfilling individual social needs or not. This made great demands on the formulation of economic policy. Planning and control must be strengthened in order to steer production towards welfare. Workplaces must be adapted to make room for weak groups and to prevent social exclusion.[24]

In the economic policy discourse of the Labour movement, then, the concept of welfare took on a meaning as a new and more social concept of growth. The concept of 'welfare' rose in importance in reports and programmes in the 1970s, and took on a very specific meaning. 'Welfare' drew on the idea that growth had historically led not only to benefits, but also to costs, and that growth should consequently be defined by its positive and negative effects in terms of increased or decreased individual security. Often used synonymously with the term 'social efficiency' (*samhällsekonomisk effektivitet*), the concept of welfare incorporated a calculation of the net value of growth, where its economic benefits were contrasted to its social costs as the other side of the equation.[25]

With these formulations, social democracy established a new framing between growth and security, one that issued from the picture of social reality and the definition of the problem of social exclusion as it had been put forward by the late 1960s critique. The formulation of welfare was founded on the concept that growth had created social costs in the form of insecurity and exclusion. Allowance must now be made for this deduction in the planning of society's economic development. In this way, welfare became a metaphor for a sustainable development that encompassed both economic and social progress and attempted to strike a new balance between the two. This was the SAP's way of trying to reestablish ideological coherence between growth and security, and find an articulation through which growth once again meant increased security and welfare for individuals.

Socialist social policies

Welfare became the guiding star in an intensified economic and social planning of the 1970s. Considerable efforts were put into social research in order to develop living standard measurements and the welfare concept as the bases for expanded social planning that would put social needs at the heart of policymaking. In 1972, the Institute for Social Research (SOFI) *Socialforskningsinstitutet* was established to take charge of the work of monitoring and quantifying living standards in order to increase political knowledge of social processes, and the concept of welfare was also put at the heart of regional policies.[26]

By the mid-1970s, then, the SAP had accepted a definition of social exclusion as a problem related to industrial growth, and as a phenomenon that required a different understanding of the interplay between economic and social development. The concept of welfare had emerged as a key metaphor in social democratic ideology, encompassing everything from economic planning to social affairs. This ideological turnaround opened up the possibility of a different outlook on the role of social policy in an industrial society, and of a social democratic discussion of how to meet the problem of social exclusion. The SAP now embraced the demands for a radically different social policy problem-solving or a structural role for social policy that had been put forward by social workers and LO economists in the late 1960s.

The late 1960s discussion of radical social policies was based on broadening the scope of problem-solving from managing the social problems of groups and individuals to influencing the structures that created these problems. Since the roots of social exclusion were in the economic system, they demanded that questions of social welfare must be integrated into the highest level of economic planning. In its most radical form, this meant an 'offensive' social policy that would replace the market economy with a kind of meta social policy, and make individual security and not economic growth the overall goal for social development.

Along with its formulation of the concept of welfare at the 1972 conference, the SAP also tried to respond to this critique by presenting a programme for the reform of social services and for a new orientation to social work that was codified as 'structural social policy'. The programme, *Socialvård i utveckling* (*Social welfare in evolution*), had been drawn up by a group appointed in 1969 as a reaction to the social workers' critique, and it was almost a blueprint of the social workers' pamphlets of the late 1960s.[27] The purpose of the report was to 'anchor social services in the Labour movement's values', and it consisted of a ten-point programme for the reform of social services, centred on the idea of participation and social citizenship:

> The transformation of social services that is to occur under the leadership of the Labour movement can be summarised in the following points: Abolish social injustices. Create a good social environment. Prevent social risks and insecurity. Build on universalism. Develop freedom and voluntariness in treatment further. Encourage the democratic development of social services. Provide all of social services with a service-directed approach. Formulate a comprehensive vision within social services. Concentrate social research on, among other issues, promoting the development of social services. Develop information about social services that will reach out to all people.[28]

The report pointed out that social democracy had always considered efforts directed at socially vulnerable groups as an 'economic investment and a positive asset', and not as a 'negative expenditure' in line with liberal traditions. But the value content of party policy towards the groups in welfare had fallen behind developments in other policy areas such as labour market policies or the social insurance system. Social democracy's approach to the social welfare clientele still built on the values of the old poor relief society. The more selective social policies outside of the social insurance system concentrated on dealing with the effects of production on vulnerable individuals, not on changing the organisation of production, and they were far from the universalism that informed other areas.[29]

The programme promised a radical rethinking of the party's standpoints on social work. To fight social exclusion and protect the weaker groups from 'one-sided demands for efficiency' the SAP would integrate social work and social services into its programme for economic democracy, and change working life to deal with the consequences of the post-war production changes on which the Labour movement was making assaults in other areas:

> Through our policy, we have steadily moved away from the original point of departure in the society of mass poverty and privilege. Today, we stand on the threshold of a social offensive. It is important to consciously take up the problems that are bound up with technical developments in industrial life ... Without a doubt, working life and its conditions will be one of the big questions of the 1970s ... [Reform] must concentrate on preventive measures within working life and the entire sphere of social services' activities.[30]

The structural role was formulated in this programme so that social work would contribute to ensuring that overarching objectives of 'equality', 'security' and 'democracy' influenced all planning. To realise these goals, social work and its experiences regarding exclusion processes would be brought into economic planning and the planning of production, work places and housing areas. In this way, all of society would be better adapted to the needs of those in the margins of society.[31] Thereby also, means such as social services and welfare would become a real force for social change, one that both created security for the individual and contributed to 'such a transformation of society that the fundamental causes of people's difficulties would be eliminated'. A structural role for social policy was, therefore, the starting point for a real 'socialistic' approach to social services. The investments made in society's most vulnerable groups would then also became part of social democracy's long-term strategy for the transformation of capitalism. This new-found social democratic emphasis on social exclusion as something rooted in production structures and not in individual weaknesses and shortcomings was underscored in a quotation from the first party leader and founding father Hjalmar Branting of the late nineteenth century, which was cited in several texts dealing with exclusion:

> all of us ought to be able to see that unfortunate, mass social phenomena have other bases than those that could be remedied through sermons about individual virtues.[32]

The Branting quote was a way of emphasising that social exclusion was a similar phenomenon to working-class poverty in historical capitalism and that the present 'social offensive' could be seen in continuity with traditional social democratic reforms. Similarly to how these historic social reforms had been understood by the Labour movement as productive investments, a structural role in welfare and services would also help to create economic efficiency and become an active 'resource-creating' policy in 1970s society, by actively preventing new social problems, putting a halt to the waste of social capital in social exclusion, and thus avoid new social costs for growth.[33]

Security, equality, democracy

The formulation of a structural role for social policy and the replacement of economic objectives in social legislation with overarching social objectives represented an important break with the strong society's ideas of social policy as primarily a means for productivity and growth. Party rhetoric saw a remarkable turnaround, by which the strong society's articulation of social policy *for* growth was replaced by an articulation of social policy as a means directed *against* growth and against the structures that had resulted in social exclusion. In this new outlook on social policy, an expanded and widened notion of security replaced growth as the objective of social reform.

In the ten-point programme, social services' old emphasis on rehabilitation and a return to production of socially vulnerable individuals was replaced with the objectives of 'security', 'equality' and 'democracy'. This was a social policy discourse in which social policy lost its productivist orientation and the notion of security was detached from notions of growth. Within this security discourse, social democracy's perspective on groups within social services also changed. Whereas the strong society's social policy had stressed the groups within social services as production factors and potential labour force reserves and the provision of security for these as part of a full commitment to production, this new security discourse focused on issues of social citizenship; their civil rights, integrity and privileges. Security was now about opportunities for an active working life and participation in production and social life, but also the right to choose not to take part in production. Along with formulations on social services' participation in social planning, the other points in the ten-point programme dealt with democratising social services, developing voluntariness in the treatment of addicts and the mentally ill, encouraging those receiving treatment to take part in decision-making processes and giving social services a 'service direction'. 'Return to production' became 'participation in the decision-making process'.[34]

The ten-point programme was the beginning of a fundamental transformation in social democracy's outlook on groups within social services and the place these occupied in party ideology. During the 1970s, a number of party working groups discussed social democracy's relationship to the handicapped, the elderly, children and youth, immigrants, recipients of public assistance, criminals, addicts and women. Party programmes and rhetoric now dealt with their rights of citizenship and the adaptation of society to their social needs.[35] In the new party programme for 1975, the new position of these groups in social democratic ideology was consolidated:

> Society should be planned to provide a favourable environment for children, one that gives all children the right to a good, harmonious childhood ... Immigrants should be given work, housing and social security on the same terms as Swedish citizens ... The elderly should be assured adequate housing as well as social care and services ... The situation of the elderly should be taken into account in the design of the overall environment ... Social services and social care should be organized around voluntariness, the individual opportunity to choose treatment alternatives and the right of participation of those involved ... Health services, rehabilitation and social services should be coordinated ... The physically disabled should be assured a living standard equal to that of other citizens. The social environment must be designed on the basis of these demands. Housing and public transportation will be adapted to these demands. Technical aids for home and work, home help and other services will be put at people's disposal. Transportation services for those who need it will be arranged. Cultural and leisure time activities will be made available to all. The right of the disabled to work will be safeguarded ... Individual integrity and the right to influence one's situation will be protected ... Social disparities and deficiencies in the environment that constitute the breeding ground for addiction will be eliminated.[36]

The SAP's rising ambitions for these groups was built on an entirely different way of looking at matters than the ambitions that the strong society's ideology had directed at the same groups as segments of a labour force reserve. Creating security for these groups was now a question of their right to care and welfare, including their right not to be productive. In this process their security was given its own intrinsic value, one that was unleashed from concerns with growth and conceptions regarding the needs of production. They should not adapt to the needs of production, but society should accommodate to their needs.

The waste of the industrial society

Consequently, the ideological changes of the 1970s saw the emergence of a discourse around social policy, where security was posited against growth, and where the purpose of social policy was rearticulated to counter growth and intervene into economic structures. In its discussion on the structural role of social policy, social democracy attempted to break with its post-war view of social problems as something related to special cases and individual symptoms, and emphasise production structures instead. This socialist approach, however, embodied a two-edged development. Where the party on the one hand expressed a deep concern with social exclusion and went to great efforts to frame it as a structural and not as an individual problem, it nevertheless found it very difficult to address the problem of social exclusion without resorting to explanations of individual failure and ended up ultimately transferring the reasons for exclusion to individual weaknesses and failures. Despite the SAP's embracing of the idea that it was the raised pace in production that was the cause of social exclusion, there was in party rhetoric also a construction of the socially excluded as a special category in society, one that could not keep up with the pace of production, that was 'weak' and 'feeble', a group that *could not be* brought back to the labour market and reintegrated into society. In a sense, the problem of social exclusion seemed to hit the very limits of social democratic ideology and the interpretation of solidarity.

This outlook on 'the weak' embodied a legacy from the social workers' and LO economists' definition of social exclusion as a problem also involving the question of a 'social heritage' by which individuals' life chances were predetermined from birth; an idea that lead to the conclusion that there were individuals who could not cope, people who could not be returned to a production system that would only exclude them again. In its rethinking of the concept of equality, the Equality Group, inspired by this idea of social heritage, argued for a concept of equality that recognised difference and compensated for weaknesses derived from unequal starting points. On the one hand this seemed like a radicalised idea of the SAP's traditional idea of equality, but on the other it drew on the recognition that there were in fact groups that were intrinsically weak, an idea the party had historically refuted. The final result of this hesitation between structure and individual in party rhetoric was that despite its emphasis on welfare, extended planning and radical social policies, the party now spoke of the socially excluded as a *de facto* underclass consisting of individuals who were fundamentally different from the working class. Party rhetoric vacillated between an emphasis on the economic structures behind exclusion and the construction of the excluded as a group of individuals who were fundamentally different from those ordinary workers, who were able to cope with the pace of production, in their failure to cope with the pace of the growth society.

This vacillation in the SAP's discourse on social exclusion characterised the 'offensive against social exclusion', which was initiated at the 1978 party congress and was something of a culmination of the 1970s radicalisation of the SAP's ambitions in the social sphere. The 1978 conference was a radical one. On the table was the LO's proposal for wage-earner funds. The conference was also the launch of the 1979 election campaign, which was social democracy's opportunity to take back government power after the lost election of 1976. However, the other big issue that the conference addressed besides the inflamed question of wage-earner funds, following one of Palme's 'portal talks', the name he gave to his core ideological speeches, was the issue of social exclusion.[37]

In Palme's highly emotionally-charged speech, the metaphor of social exclusion acquired a slightly different meaning than in the discussion on welfare and structural social policies as attempts to meet the structural causes of exclusion. In the speech, social exclusion was a description that encompassed the entire spectrum of problematic groups in the social reality of the 1970s: people who were incapacitated or in early retirement, the homeless, the young unemployed, single mothers, worn-out industrial workers, displaced immigrants whose children grew up in the rootlessness of exile, and those living in tough suburban neighbourhoods. Indeed, Palme stressed the difficulty of defining who was excluded, since exclusion was a complex process created by tendencies that he saw as inherent in industrial capitalism; insecurity, unemployment, alienation and abuse. Thus, 'exclusion' extended over a number of groups, from individuals with very specific problems, such as heroin addicts, to more universal categories, such as suburban dwellers, single mothers and immigrants. Exclusion was a process controlled by insecurity, loneliness and alienation, against which social democracy had to be continually on guard, since it threatened large groups in society:

> We usually speak of exclusion. It is a tough word. It means that someone has more or less been left out. Left out of society. Left out of the labour market. Left out of school. Left out of the community. It is impossible to easily and precisely define who is socially excluded or to determine how many have been left out of the community. Studies indicate that the number of alcoholics is estimated to be between 200,000 and 300,000 or five percent of the population ... The number of drug addicts is estimated to be between 10,000 and 15,000, of which 2,000 are estimated to be addicted to heroin. Every year, 2,000 people between the ages of 16 and 34 are granted early retirement pensions. In Stockholm, there are about 5,000 homeless people, who hang out in service flats, shelters, in the parks and on the streets ... There are people who are losing their footing ... What happens if their jobs are taken away from them? ... If young people cannot live up to all the demands placed on them?[38]

The common denominator for all of these groups of excluded individuals was their alienation in the growth society. The excluded people had no *value* in a society that measured progress by productivity and income. 'More and more people feel as if they are on the outside – that they have no value or importance', wrote the Social Democrats the same year in a bill to parliament.[39] In his speech, Palme spoke of exclusion as an 'open sore in modern industrial societies', created by post-war population resettlements, inadequate social environments and an all-too-difficult working life. 'Competitive society's barriers of strength and efficiency' divested human beings of their self-esteem. People are 'interchangeable'. 'No one is interested in skills, just in productive capacity.' The excluded were the low productive, the underachievers, the people who lived in fear of losing their jobs and of not being able to cope.[40]

These were phenomena that affected large groups in society. At the same time, Palme spoke of social exclusion as a rather narrow phenomenon that primarily had to do with alcohol and drug abuse. The filmmaker Stefan Jarl's film, *Ett anständigt liv* (*A dignified life*), was released during the 1979 election campaign. The film had a huge impact on the Swedish Labour movement. It conveyed a striking picture of a harshening social reality that seemed very far from the dream of a people's home that knew no privileged and no outcasts. In the film, two homeless Stockholm vagabonds, Kenta and Stoffe, put a face on social exclusion and the harsh conditions of survival in a Stockholm underworld. The film ended with Stoffe's death of a heroin overdose at the T-centralen subway station.[41]

Kenta and Stoffe first appeared in Stefan Jarl's 1968 film *Dom kallar oss mods* (*They call us mods*). In the film, that was very much part of the late 1960s debate on the shortcomings of the SAP and of the growing left wing critique of the collectivism of the Swedish welfare state, Kenta and Stoffe represented the late 1960s counterculture to welfare statism and the counterculture of social democracy. Kenta and Stoffe were filmed smoking marijuana (this fed into a social democratic debate on the harmful effects of the Americanisation of Swedish popular culture) and making fun of the Swedish working man with the song, 'petty nine-to-fivers, petty nine-to-fivers, are funny to behold' (*små knegarna, små knegarna, är lustiga att se*).[42] The song was a travesty of a traditional Swedish children's rhyme that goes *little frogs, little frogs, are funny to behold ...* (*små grodorna, små grodorna, är lustiga att se*) which is sung and danced around the maypole on midsummer's eve. The film, to put it bluntly, was a kick in the face of idealisations of Swedish society. By 1978, when Stefan Jarl took his camera back to document what had happened to Kenta and Stoffe in the intervening ten years, they were no longer representatives of a youthful counterculture but down-and-out outcasts on society's margins. In Palme's talk to the conference in 1978, Kenta and Stoffe became the personifications of the social price of growth.

Olof Palme was clearly very struck by the film, and he seems to have experienced the problem of social exclusion, drug abuse and alienation as a central ideological dilemma. His descriptions of social exclusion were indignant, compassionate. Palme clearly saw the problem of drug abuse, social exclusion and alienation in welfare capitalism as a crucial concern of the industrial society, to the point of being a failure of social democratic ideology. Stefan Jarl's film was rapidly transformed into material for a study circle for the ABF (The Workers' Educational Association) the traditional heart of workers' education. Palme wrote the introduction to the study material and gave several radio speeches and television interviews in connection with the film.[43] In an interview with the legendary TV journalist Herbert Söderström, Palme spoke of social exclusion as a new and unpleasant version of the industrial proletariat:

> There is no other social evil that worries me as much as this does ... It affects the whole western world. It doesn't lead to unrest because there is the welfare state ... It is the low productive being eliminated, the unprofitable. It brings down the pressure of wages ... It is a kind of decay, from within, of the industrial world. I can't think ... well it's a big group. It's too easy to say that this is the fault of capitalism, overthrow capitalism and we will be rid of it. But I mean that if we want to live in a civilized society some of the material growth we create has to be devoted to thoroughly dealing with these problems.[44]

In Palme's discussion on the socially excluded, a break with the strong society's approach to the socially problematic groups clearly stands out. The excluded did not represent potential labour force resources – they were on the lowest level of the industrial society's hierarchy. Applying the parable that Palme used in his speech, they were the waste of the industrial society, its exhausted production factors. 'It is a nightmare vision. It is people as industrial refuse.'[45] The metal worker, whose words Palme borrowed for his speech, said:

> I have slaved hard all my life and now, when I am worn out and sick, I'm tossed on the garbage heap.[46]

It was these feelings of worthlessness and alienation outside of production that united Kenta and Stoffe with handicapped people, single mothers, immigrants, suburban dwellers and worn-out industrial workers in social democracy's image of exclusion. Social insurances, active labour market policies and pensions aside, they were left with a pervasive feeling of worthlessness. That was the essence of social exclusion. Now, instead of representing potential production resources, the excluded individuals represented production costs. This way of looking at things appeared again in Palme's indignant description of industrial society's refuse; refuse is a worn-out resource, something that has served its purpose and is no longer useful. Taking care of these weak, worn-out groups was closer to being a societal cost, the kind 'one can afford', to quote Alva Myrdal from her speech to the 1969 congress, than a prerequisite for growth.

In the mid-1970s, the LO proposed that social services and social work should be considered as production costs since they were concerned with spillover costs that industry placed on society. Olof Palme also took up this matter in his speech to the 1978 congress. Alongside the struggle for wage-earner funds and economic democracy, social democracy must also fight the social structures that Palme saw as a modern reminder of the class society, particularly in a time when the political and economic climate was getting tougher. By making companies responsible for social care, in the same way that the Labour movement had stressed economic democracy and the work environment, social exclusion could be addressed within the production and its externalised costs internalised.[47] But no such demand ever came from the Swedish Labour movement. Instead, the discussion of both the SAP and the LO stopped at a plea for working-class solidarity with society's weakest members. The emphasis on structural solutions in the form of radical social problem-solving or some level of corporate tax for social exclusion was replaced with a discourse on 'fraternity', 'everyday solidarity', and 'community cooperation'. The exclusion processes would be stopped through trade union initiated social work at work places, fraternal production groups, and collaboration between local union representatives and social workers.[48]

Palme concluded his speech at the 1978 congress by reformulating the old metaphor of the people's home to match the social reality of the 1970s: 'Per Albin could have added: A good home does not know of social exclusion.'[49]

> We must never accept individuals being looked upon as outcasts and cursed ... I have said it before: there must never be them and us; there is only we![50]

However, Palme's plea for working-class solidarity departed in the recognition that in fact there was a group in society that was fundamentally different from the working class. Consequently, the discussion on social exclusion took a turn whereby it ultimately dealt more with 'solidarity with the weak' than with influencing the organisation of production and economic structures.

The limits of security

Social democracy's interpretation of social exclusion thus had a critical limit. In its ideas of radical social problem-solving that was directed to economic structures and strove to prevent social exclusion, social democracy took in essential parts of the critique it had met with in the late 1960s. The ten-point programme incorporated the idea of a structural role for social policy, and the radicalisation of the concept of security that the social workers and LO economists had demanded. However, there was a crucial difference between the discourse that social democracy had now established around social policy and the discourse of the late 1960s. This difference was the standing of the concept of growth.

In the interpretation of the critique of the late 1960s, the objective of radical social policies was to replace growth as a hegemonic goal in long-term planning with individual security, and ultimately, to replace the market economic system with a kind of structural social planning. In social democracy's interpretation, the structural role of social policy was, rather, about developing social policy's position in the capitalist economy and strengthening the objective of security, but it was never about replacing growth. In its incorporation of the articulation of the critique of the radical left, social democracy thereby also eliminated its most radical framing.

This discrepancy between the late 1960s discourse and the more modest form that the social democratic interpretation took in spite of its rhetoric about socialist social services, led to some internal debate. At the 1972 party conference, critical voices objected that the programme did not actually address the causes of exclusion. Rather than use new means to attend to new social problems, it was time to initiate a debate on the capitalist system and its 'ruthless exploitation' of human beings.[51]

The structural role of social policy was never given concrete form in social democratic policymaking. The SAP contented itself with referring the question of a new role for social policy to further investigation in a parliamentary committee. Nor did it appear that anyone believed that a socialist role for social services would lead to the elimination of social problems, exclusion or the need for social services in the long run. If anything, party programmes stressed that social services were becoming more and more important in a modern industrial society with its high rate of production.[52] The formulation of a structure-influencing role for social policy was a discourse limited to a question of reforming social services and getting rid of the poor relief label they had been given in the late 1960s, thereby accommodating critique while at the same time, silencing its most radical articulations. In a sense, Palme's call to take on social exclusion as the most pressing social issue was also a statement on the fundamental limit of the role of politics to provide individual security. Social exclusion, to him, was after all not something that was rooted only in economic structures, but had its causes in abstract and intangible individual feelings of insecurity and alienation. His speech to the party conference in 1978 also stated that the party had to realise 'the fundamental limits. We can't reform away feelings of fear and insecurity'.[53]

Social reform and social work

The main result of the SAP's formulation of a structural role for social policy was that an intense policy production began in the social and economic administration with how to operationalise the overarching social goals of security, equality, and democracy into planning models and concrete policies. A lot of this work was channelled to the parliamentary committee in charge of developing a new social legislation. On the basis of the SAP's ten-point programme, this Committee was asked to develop the structural role and work out how 'security', 'equality' and 'democracy' could actually be posited against growth as goals for social policy and social planning.[54]

What emerged from the Committee was a radically different idea of problem-solving in social policy than the rather technocratic outlook that had characterised policymaking in the strong society, and one that was very concerned with the limits to security in terms of the scope of social reform. For the Committee, social reform was an extremely unpredictable process. In a time where social problems had arisen as the unforeseen consequences of previous policy, the purpose of the problem-solving process seemed deeply uncertain. Social problems were not the remains of an older societal stage but rather issues that were continually reproduced and re-emerged as the unforeseen consequences of previous planning and reform. It was questionable even if policymakers, and the social democratic government, were sufficiently in touch with social reality to provide adequate definitions of social problems. Exclusion took place in a reality that was far from policymakers, through processes that were difficult to define, quantify, and operationalise.[55]

Because of the unpredictable nature of the dynamics of social exclusion and social problems, the Committee suggested that new social legislation should be designed as a flexible and long-term, all-embracing goal formulation, one that would clearly set forth overarching values of security, equality and democracy as the core values of social policy, but leave the operationalisation of these overarching objectives to local authorities who could adapt them to local conditions, and ultimately to social workers in the field. The goals had to be general because the planning process could not foresee what problems might arise in an uncertain future that could be expected to once again bring about unexpected social problems. The legislation should provide the legal framework for flexible and decentralised problem-solving, in order to target local social problems. Since new understandings of social problems could no doubt be expected in the future, along with changes in values (the Committee straddled the parliamentary takeover in 1976) the goals had to be loosely formulated. Further, to be able to cover the unpredictable nature of social development, the goals of a new social legislation also had to exist in a sort of continual reformulation process, where experiences from 'the field' would constantly be taken into account in local implementation of the overarching objectives of the law. The Committee believed that socio-political planning must continually take stock of new social problems that could crop up as the unforeseen consequences of previous decisions; social policy's goals must, therefore, be long-term and comprehensive enough to remain in place, as well as flexible enough to integrate new problem images into future societal circumstances. Security, equality and democracy were broad, general goals on which one could assume there would be consensus in the future. It was these comprehensive objectives that would steer social services' participation in social planning and constitute the foundation for new social legislation. In its main report, the Committee did not provide any more concrete substance on the social goals and social welfare's structure-influencing role. Instead, it stated that the concrete substance of these all-embracing roles must be formulated on the basis of the knowledge that would continually come to light about social processes in practical social work in the field.[56]

The basis for radical and structural social policy problem-solving was therefore, ultimately, to be found in the fieldwork of social workers. The Committee identified *community work* as the central means to fight social exclusion in communities and neighbourhoods that were hard to reach with conventional policies. The purpose of community work was to counteract exclusion processes and, using knowledge from the field about exclusion, fill the law's overarching objectives with substance and prevent new exclusion processes. This knowledge would then constitute the basis for analyses of social needs for planning at all levels: in the preparations of plans for social services; in technical and economic planning; in the construction of housing estates and in the planning of traffic, infrastructure and industry. Social exclusion would be neutralised through social workers in the field. The responsibility for implementing the structure-influencing role, therefore, was laid at the feet of social workers in a kind of bottom-up social planning.[57]

Community work emerged internationally in the 1960s and 1970s as a strongly radicalised form of social work, that turned the perspective of social work from implementing central policy decisions in the field to a kind of grass-roots perspective where social reform started from below, with social workers in the field engaging excluded groups and 'raising their awareness' about their economic and social situation and their position on the margins of society. Community work, then, was a reform policy that placed the social worker at the centre of the process and started from the social worker's understanding of local social problems, not from political descriptions of social reality and the social problems. Community work had its origins in the Latin American revolution, where social work was used as a project of political mobilisation in poor areas. Paolo Freire's book on radical social work, *Pedagogy of indignation*, was translated into Swedish in 1972 under the title *Pedagogik för förtryckta* and was highly influential among left-wing social workers. Community work also took on a central role in the war on poverty in the United States, where it became a way of reaching excluded groups in big-city ghettos. In Sweden, experiments with community work were carried out in the early 1970s in the dilapidated council estates of Rosengård and Östergård in Malmö, and Aspudden in Stockholm.[58]

This trust in the fieldwork and local prerogatives of social workers was a major step away from how the SAP had historically thought about social reform and social work. In the 1930s, a central tenet of the universal social policies that were developed by the minister of social affairs Gustav Möller was that the individual should be protected from the stigmatising bureaucratic procedures of means-testing and from the power of individual social bureaucrats. Social workers, in those days, where seen as representatives of a bourgeois society, and their activities as part of a repressive strategy through which the old society kept the working class on the leash. The SAP of the 1970s put its faith in a new generation of social workers who were presumed to share the values of the working class, to the point that it trusted them with knowing how best to provide security for groups in society that the party itself felt deeply alienated from. Social workers could do what social democracy couldn't – reduce the insecurity and sufferings of the weakest. This new role for social workers and the centrality of social were codified in the implementation of the new Social Welfare Act (*Socialtjänstlagen, SoL*) in 1982. The new legislation was prepared, from 1976 onwards, by the Liberal government, but it was pushed through by the SAP as it came back into power in 1982. The law took the form of skeleton law that formulated the goals of social policy as security, equality and democracy, but left considerable scope for local solutions and community work. The law, then, was the final realisation of the changed values around democratisation and participation that the social workers put forward in the late 1960s, and it gave them the influence over social planning and social work that they had sought.[59]

In retrospect, the implementation of the new social welfare act in 1982 has been seen as an important part of the change of the Swedish model in the 1980s and 1990s, because its loose legal framework permitted an erosion of social rights and standards in the 1990s recession. The flexibility of the framework legislation and the scope it allowed for local solutions put the content of social policy in the hands of local government, that in the period from the 1990s has been increasingly squeezed for resources. The power to define standards went from the national level to a question of the judgement of the individual social worker. Thus, the legislation underwent some trajectory from the suggestions for a new and radical form of social policy for individual empowerment in the late 1960s. In the 1990s, the law was again compared to the old poor relief, as a law that, with new means, was directed towards the 'weak' in society.

By this time the central policy problem had changed. In the 1960s and 1970s, the problem in the focus of politics was to meet what seemed like a threatening and deeply unpredictable process of social change, and meet the problems of social exclusion. But from the latter half of the 1970s the problem was not to counter a worrisome social transformation, but to confront a suddenly dramatically altered economic reality. This was obvious already when the act was passed in 1982. By then, its purpose of facing up to the problem of social exclusion had been complemented by another objective, that of providing a decentralised legal framework that would allow for social ambitions to be adapted to narrowing economic circumstances. The purpose of meeting the social costs for growth had been replaced by the purpose of meeting the economic costs for security.[60]

Concluding remarks

Social reality seemed to catch up with social democratic ideology in the 1970s. The late 1960s critique and the image it put forward of a social underworld of exclusion and marginalisation created deep-seated tensions in the strong society's ideology. Growth and security became extremely antagonistic goals in what must be called a crisis of social democratic ideology. The 1970s took the form of a conflict-ridden and often contradictory labouring of ideology, concerned with how social democracy would take in the problem of social exclusion and rethink ideology around the fact that everyone could not, manifestly, be included in the growth society. The notion of welfare was an attempt to solve the conflict between the notions of growth and security, and the offensive against social exclusion another attempt to raise the ideological ceiling around this issue. In a sense, as is particularly clear in Olof Palme's thinking, social exclusion seemed to address the very limit of social democratic ideology. How would one address a group in society that for various reasons could not or would not be part of the productive society, and who despite the ground gained in terms of social reform seemed to suffer from abstract and intangible feelings of rootlessness and alienation? Ultimately, the SAP's discourse on social exclusion left the terrain of capitalist structures and ended up in such individualised descriptions of what distinguished the socially excluded, the 'weak', from the rest of the working class. There was a defeatist idea in this, despite the radicalised concept of security as welfare, inclusion and social citizenship that informed 1970s ideology, a defeatist conception that social change was so complicated and so unpredictable that there were fundamental limits to what reform politics could achieve. The SAP's handing over of the problem of social exclusion to social workers in the field testified to this defeatist conception. There were insecurities that went beyond universalist social policies and solidary wage bargaining, and could only be addressed in the relationships between people, far below the level of party politics and government. In a way, the SAP seemed to come to terms with a fundamentally dichotomous outlook in society, an outlook in which there were two worlds; one world populated by social democrats who worked hard and made their voice heard in party conferences and local councils, and an underworld of people on the margins who did not participate in any sense of the word. There was a strong sense of detachment between these two, and the division, somehow, also seemed to recognise that social democracy was perhaps not the best suited to speak for the latter. When Palme spoke to the party conference on social exclusion in 1978, he relied on Stefan Jarl's film and on newspaper clippings and other documentary reports for his speech. For a comfortably middle-class party conference he drew up a kind of cabinet of the different personalities of social exclusion. This detached description of social reality, compassionate as it was, stands in glaring contrast to 1950s social democratic accounts of personal experiences of the poor relief system. Social democracy was simply not enough in touch with this part of social reality.[62]

Notes

1 Club of Rome, 1976, *The limits to growth*, Paris; Friman 2002 p. 64f.

2 Ayres 1998 p. 104; Arndt 1987 p. 89f; Hirsch, F., 1995, *The socials limits to growth*, Routledge, London. In 1971 an OECD report argued that the concept of welfare was a better definition of economic progress than the term growth, and suggested that welfare and quantitative so-called social indicators should replace GDP in international economic planning: OECD, 1971, *The Brooks-report. Science, growth and society*, Paris. Whereas this report had a certain influence on the Swedish discussion, the OECD's work with social indicators also drew on the pioneering work on social indicators carried out by the Swedish Committee on Low Income and the work primarily of Sten Johansson.

3 Elander, I., 1978, *Det nödvändiga och det önskvärda*, Arkiv, Lund; Holmberg, C., 1988, *Längtan till landet, civilisationskritik och framstegsvisioner i 1970–talets regionalpolitiska debatt*, Arkiv, Lund.

4 Friman 2002; Anshelm, J., 1995, *Socialdemokratin och miljöfrågan*, Symposion, Stockholm; Andersson, J., 2006, 'Alva Myrdal and the construction of Swedish futures studies 1967–1972', *International review of social history*, 51, 2006, pp. 277–295.

5 Stråth 1998.

6 Benner 1997 pp. 109, 125f.

7 Lundberg-Petersen 1999 p. 100; Stråth 1998 p. 94f.; Florin, C. and Nilsson, B., 1999, 'Something in the nature of a bloodless revolution, how new gender relations became gender equality policies in Sweden in the 1960s and 70s', in Torstendahl, R. (ed.), *State policy and the gender system in the two German states and Sweden 1945–1989*, Studia Historica Upsaliensia, Uppsala; Heclo 1987; Hinnfors, J., 1992, *Familjepolitik*, Arkiv, Lund; Korpi, W., 1983, *The democratic class struggle*, Walter Kegan, London; Olsson 1993.

8 In the *miljonprogrammet*, the SAP resolved to build one million apartments in the suburbs of Stockholm, Göteborg and Malmö in the 10–year period between 1964 and 1974. The programme resulted in the creation of suburbs such as Skärholmen in Stockholm or Rosengård in Malmö, areas that in the 1960s were seen as modern and efficient housing for the working class, but that rapidly deteriorated into working-class poverty. In recent decades, these suburbs have also become deeply segregated in ethnic terms. See Molina, I., 2000, 'City template, multi-ethnic metropolitan Stockholm', Partnership for multiethnic integration, Umeå.

9 SAP 1969; SAP 1972a, *Jämlikhet, allas deltagande i politik och arbetsliv*; 1972b, *Socialvård i utveckling*.

10 Palme 1971 'Tillväxt, balans, jämlikhet', *Vårt ekonomiska läge*, p. 35.

11 Palme 1971 p. 39.

12 Palme 1972, 'Socialdemokratin i Europa, starkare än någonsin' (Social democracy in Europe, stronger than ever), *Tiden*, 64 7/8 p. 392; Club of Rome 1976; Andersson 2006.

13 Palme 1972.

14 Letter from Olof Palme to Willy Brandt and Bruno Kreisky, March 17 1972, in Brandt, W., Kreisky, B. and Palme, O., 1975, *Briefe und Gespräche*, Europeische Verlagsanstalt, Frankfurt, p. 19.

15 Palme 1972 p. 392.

16 Palme 1972; Brandt, Kreisky and Palme 1975 p. 19.

17 Palme 1971 p. 39.
18 *Aftonbladet* October 4 1974 p. 10f.
19 SAP 1972 conference protocol p. 16.
20 SAP 1972a p. 21 f.
21 SAP 1972a pp. 23, 28; SAP 1972 conference protocol pp. 148–157.
22 LO-SAP 1972, *Näringspolitisk rapport*, p. 5.
23 LO-SAP 1972 p. 31.
24 SAP 1972a; LO-SAP 1972 pp. 15, 31, 57–62, 70f. See SAP 1974, *Välfärd och arbete åt alla*; SAP 1975a, *En demokratisk hushållning*, pp. 40, 64; LO-SAP 1978, *Sysselsättningspolitik inför 1980–talet.*
25 LO-SAP 1972 p. 31; see also SAP 1972a p. 21.
26 Ds In 1972:17 p. 56f; *Forskningsberedningen* (Swedish council of science) 1968; Statsverkspropositionen 1969 p. 346; Ds U 1971:4 pp. 19, 25, s. 32; Ds S 1973:1; Ds S 1973:8, pp. 6, 21; Johansson 1979 p. 23f.
27 SAP 1969 conference protocol p. 449; SAP 1972b. The party also held *rådslag*, grass-roots conversations, on social services in 1969 and 1971; see SAP archives F 10H vols 36 (1969) and F 10H vols 47, 48 (1971).
28 SAP 1972 conference protocol p. 325.
29 SAP 1972b p. 9.
30 SAP 1972b p. 10.
31 SAP 1972 conference protocol p. 325.
32 See SAP parliament bill in opposition 1976/77:1097 and LO 1976, *Fackföreningsrörelsen och socialpolitiken*, p. 14.
33 SAP 1972b p. 19; LO 1976 p. 106.
34 SAP 1972b p. 39; Aspling, S., 1970, *Socialpolitiskt reformarbete för ökad jämställdhet*; Aspling 1971, *Socialpolitiken – trygghetspolitiken.*
35 SAP 1975b, *Trygghet och rättvisa åt de handikappade*, pp. 9–11; SAP 1975c, *Socialdemokratin och den unga generationen*; SAP 1978, *Invandrarpolitiskt program*; SAP 1983, *Kommunal socialpolitik.*
36 Party programme, 1975d: *Partiprogram och kommunalt principprogram fastställda efter 1975 års kongress* (selective). After the parliamentary shift in 1976 the SAP put a series of parliamentary bills for rights for these groups; see bills in parliament 1978/79:667, 1978/79:600, 1978/79:1050 and 1976/77:1519.
37 The speech was reprinted in Palme, O., 1987, *Politik är att vilja*, pp. 162–174.
38 SAP 1978 conference protocol p. 933.
39 SAP 1978 conference protocol p. 23.
40 SAP 1978 conference protocol pp. 933–935.
41 Jarl, S., 1978, *Ett anständigt liv*, Norstedts, Stockholm.
42 Jarl, S., 1968, *Dom kallar oss mods*, Aldus Bonnier, Stockholm.
43 Jarl 1978. It might be added that every Swede of my generation has been shown this film in school as part of information campaigns against drugs.
44 Palme in interview, *Aktuellt frågar*, November 11 1979. See printout in the Olof Palme archive. I have shortened the original quote somewhat. The full quote in Swedish is: *Inget samhällsproblem oroar mig så mycket som detta ... det finns inte en ort i landet som är så liten att den inte har ett A-lag. Det finns inte en parksnutt ... Det är ju likadant i hela Västeuropa, över hela världen. Det har att göra med arbetslösheten. För tio år sedan hade man sagt, att får vi en så stor arbetslöshet då blir det revolution. Det blev det inte alltså, för att man hade ju matkuponger, socialbidrag. Så kan man säga att ja, det här är de lågproduktiva som slås ut, de olönsamma. Det blir dessutom*

dämpade lönekrav om man har en sån här armé ... Jag tror att det är en förruttnelse-process, inifrån alltså, i industrivärlden. Jag kan inte tro ... trasproletariat blir det alltså en stor grupp. Det är väl enkelt att säga att det här är kapitalismens fel, avskaffa kapitalismen så försvinner det här. Det är för enkelt, därför att det är mycket allvarligare processer. Det har att göra med lönsamhetskrav, med effektivitet, med teknisk utveckling och allt sådant som att människor skjutsas ut och drivs allt djupare i misären. Men jag menar, att ska vi få ett civiliserat samhälle så måste en del av den tillväxt vi kan skapa gå på djupet och röja upp de här problemen.

45 SAP 1978 conference protocol p. 936.

46 SAP 1978 conference protocol p. 934.

47 LO 1976 p. 57f.

48 SAP 1978 conference protocol pp. 933–941; LO 1976.

49 SAP 1978 conference protocol p. 941. The original people's home quote in Per Albin Hansson's speech in 1928 was 'The good home knows no privileged or rejected, no favourites and no stepchildren' (*Det goda hemmet känner icke till några privilegierade eller tillbakasatta, inga kelgrisar och inga styvbarn*).

50 SAP 1978 conference protocol p. 936.

51 SAP 1972 conference protocol p. 361f.

52 SAP 1969 p. 14f; SAP 1972b; SOU 1974:39 p. 95.

53 Palme speech 1978.

54 Socialstyrelsen (Board of social affairs) 1971, *Sociala mål*; 1972, *Sociala mål, social planering*.

55 SOU 1974:39.

56 SOU 1974:39; Socialstyrelsen 1971 p. 7.

57 Denvall, V. and Salonen, T., 1997, *Välfärdens operatörer, om social planering i brytningstid*, Boréa, Umeå; Lund, p. 56; Socialstyrelsen 1971 p. 118f.

58 Holgersson 1998 p. 124; O'Connor 2001.

59 Holgersson 1998 p. 81f; Elmér, Å, 1993, *Svensk socialpolitik*, Liber, Stockholm, p. 208.

60 SOU 1974:39 pp. 513, 530; SOU 1974:40 p. 87.

61 Johansson 2001; Denvall 1994.

62 I am grateful to Lena Hjelm-Wallen for recounting to me that Palme, because of the way he as party leader travelled around Sweden in the election campaigns in the 1970s and 1980s, came to feel a personal connection with many of the people who slept on the benches of the parks where he came to give speeches. He considered them his test audience.

5
The cost of security

Introduction

The radicalisation of the SAP's ideology in the social sphere in the 1970s broke with the strong society's growth orientation. Growth, as the overarching goal of social policy, became security. The ideological preoccupation with the prevention and management of social exclusion, and the strengthened emphasis on security, was an attempt to detach from the productivism of the post-war period and give social goals a value of their own. The rearticulation of growth as a social force for welfare was social democracy's response to the critique of the late 1960s, and can be seen as an effort to recreate a harmonious framing between 'growth' and 'security', that once again set them as compatible goals.

The ideology that emerged in the 1970s was, however, a conflict-ridden one. Despite the attempts, on the surface of party rhetoric and programmes, to break with the growth orientation of the previous decades and articulate a 'more social' ideology, social democracy never did let go of the objective of growth, but continued to defend it as the fundamental condition for security.

The conflict between growth and security and the debate over which should have precedence over the other intensified throughout the 1970s, parallel to fundamental changes in the surrounding world. With the stagnation of industrial growth and increasing price movements in international markets, the Labour movement's preoccupation with growth's social consequences was gradually replaced by the insight that the golden era of economic expansion had come to an end. The SAP's fear of the social consequences of growth was replaced with the fear of no growth. This concern with an eroding material base lead to new articulations of growth and reappraisals of its central role in the welfare state. Parallel with the SAP's discussion on the social content of growth, its newfound notion of welfare, and its rising ambitions in social policy, a discourse that increasingly concentrated on the active creation of growth was finding voice. To this end, the concept of growth never lost its hegemonic position, but rather it was strengthened through the developments of the decade. The tensions within social democratic ideology took the form of a vacillation between the emphasis, on the one hand, on growth's consequences in terms of insecurity and the need for a widened concept of growth that took social effects into account, and, on the other, the defence of growth as the continued basis for security, and a concept of growth that was, rather, narrowing. The intensification of social democratic economic policy and coordinated measures for strengthened economic planning (which in Chapter 4 was discussed as an economic offensive in reaction to the experiences of social exclusion) also included a reaction to the dwindling growth of the late 1960s. It was thus a two-edged ideological development, responding to a situation that was sometimes described by social democrats as the 'two-front war of growth'.[1]

Behind the 1970s talk of individual social rights and overarching social goals, there was thus a fundamental continuity with the strong society's framings concerning the primacy of economic growth. Nevertheless, the 1970s saw a seachange in social democracy's understanding of *how* growth should be created. The 1970s economic offensive contained the formulation of a social democratic industrial policy with the purpose of exerting greater influence on investments in the Swedish export industry.[2] The development around the creation of industrial policy has been described as a break with functional socialism, and the SAP's historical concentration on the control of the consumer side and distribution, rather than intervention into production. The formulation of industrial policy meant that the Labour movement took on the problems of Swedish industry, and it brought with it a shift of focus from the concentration in the 1950s and 1960s on the public sector, to a focus on the increasingly problem-laden export sector.[3] The idea of controlling industrial investment was an important break with post-war ideology, and indeed it has often been seen as the step away from the corporatism of the model, that brought on the conflict with Swedish employers and industry by the end of the decade. It was coupled with the offensive for economic democracy and wage-earner funds that also aimed to increase control over profits. However, the formulation of industrial policy broke with functional socialism in a second sense, because it also meant a break with social democracy's emphasis on social reforms and public services as the route to an efficient society. The shift of focus from public expenditure to industry investments meant a reinterpretation of the Labour movement's idea of the significance of public expenditure for the creation of growth. This reinterpretation took place parallel to the continued turn in social policies towards society's 'weakest'. These changes led up to the gradual emergence of a new economic language around the public sector and around social reform in Swedish social democracy, an economic language that increasingly distinguished between 'productive' and 'unproductive' resources, between production and consumption, and between productive groups in the economy and those groups that social democracy now deemed as weak and unproductive. The SAP's ideas of social policy as a productive investment were replaced by more and more frequent references to social policy as an expense. Social policy was no longer, as Gunnar Myrdal once stated, a matter of creation of resources, but a matter of the redistribution and transfer of resources from productive to unproductive.

A burden for productive resources or a dynamic, liberating force?

From the late 1960s, the SAP's preoccupation with the problem of social exclusion and the social cost of growth coexisted with a growing preoccupation with the economic costs of social reform in the party's economic discourse. In the course of the 1970s, the articulations that were formulated in response to the critique of the late 1960s were gradually silenced in the party's ideological debate.

Dating back to the late 1960s concern with the first signs of economic stagnation and inflationary pressure, the SAP's economic worldview was starting to tremble. The confidence in the Swedish economy's potential to fund new social reforms gradually gave way to a worldview of a shrinking material foundation, which placed stricter limitations on reform politics. The 1967 conference, which had launched the debate on economic democracy and social exclusion, was also triggered by the declining export figures of Swedish industry, traditionally exceptionally export-dependent. This was a central motivation for drawing up the economic offensive. The economic guidelines that were put forth by the party executive included recommendations for a tougher rationalisation pace and an intensified structural change in the Swedish economy, as the primary means to meet these initial problems.[4]

The recommendation for increased rationalisation clashed with the heated debate on social exclusion within the Labour movement. This led to a somewhat paradoxical development in SAP ideology, where the idea of increased social ambitions in order to meet social needs that had arisen as consequences of economic growth was replaced by an emphasis on more growth, to meet these increased social demands. The party defended its recommendation for intensified structural change and rationalisation with the argument that problems of insecurity and the increased social demands required more resources, to pay for more security. The increased social ambitions of the 1970s required more resources. The 1968 economic report connected the urgency of rationalisation with the new development in social policy vis-à-vis the groups in society that were outside of production. The fact that ambitions for groups such as the 'excluded' and the 'weak' were on the increase meant that socio-political activities were now less about social reforms to tie working groups to the labour market, and more about transfers from society's productive groups to its 'non-productive ones'.[5] Creating security for unproductive groups required an increase in production. Thus, increased security for these groups required an intensified structural transformation and increased production in trade and industry. This framing grew in strength in economic policy during the 1970s, in spite of the contemporaneous discussion on growth's social consequences.

The 1972 economic report, the same report that had redefined the purpose of economic policy as 'welfare' and dismissed the concept of growth as something that led to social exclusion, also advocated increased rationalisation in order to increase economic productivity to pay for continued social reforms. In its discussion of a strengthened economic planning that would increase the control over growth's social effects, the report had defined the purpose of economic policy as 'social efficiency', which meant an expansion that would not lead to exclusion and that would put 'welfare' rather than production profits at the centre of policy. But at the same time, the report included a lengthy discussion on the need for increased economic productivity. The increasing fluctuations in the international economy made Swedish industry, with its great dependence on foreign trade, more and more vulnerable. In spite of the party's welfare debate, the programme stated that it was the role of economic policy to create growth in an increasingly difficult economic situation and thereby create the economic resources that would make possible the continued social reform policy to which the Labour movement was devoting so much time and energy.[6] Therefore, economic policy must assume industry's problems and actively intervene in the branches hard-hit by crisis, for the purpose of raising competitiveness and productivity. An efficient economy was, after all, the prerequisite of individual security.

> Only the full exploitation of our productive resources will make it possible for us to carry out our reform policy and transform society![7]

The antagonism between this focus on increased productivity and intensified structural change, and social democracy's discussion of social exclusion as the consequence of post-war rationalisation, was manifest. The party's formulations on the urgency of growth and rationalisation were to be found in the very same reports that seemed to turn the page on the SAP's post-war growth ideology. Nor did it go unnoticed. A series of motions that protested the report's concentration on growth and demanded more discussion on the antagonism between the market economy system and social needs were introduced at the conference in 1972, where the report was presented.[8]

The party debate around the conflict between welfare and individual security, on the one hand, and growth and rationalisation on the other, gave rise to rather pointed refutations from the Economic Policy Committee and from the party executive. The party executive dismissed the conference debate, with reference to changed 'realities', namely, an economic situation marked by shortages and by new developments in the world economy that were particularly worrisome for the small and export-dependent Swedish economy. These realities required a more stringent economic policy and intensified economic modernisation. Anything else would be utopic.[9] Again, the argument was that the creation of resources for the heightened social ambitions of socially vulnerable groups required production increases that could not be met without continued rationalisation.[10] To end any further debate, the executive stated that all raised objections had been addressed and that it could not be argued that the Labour movement had not taken the critique of growth seriously. After all, the party had devoted much effort to the discussion on growth's social content and on integrating the concept of welfare into social democratic ideology. The SAP had taken on the problems of insecurity and exclusion. In addition, according to the party executive, the Labour movement had never viewed growth as a goal in and of itself, but rather as the means to achieving the social ends that were the principal values of social democratic ideology. An increased emphasis on rationalisation and strengthened efforts for structural change were not ends in themselves, but should be understood, rather, as means to security.

> The social democratic policy has always been focused on measures intended to increase welfare ... In times of considerable material shortages, the contributions have, for obvious reasons, been directed to the creation of the material conditions that are needed to ... give every individual the possibility of a rich, meaningful life. When an important instrument for this is a rational economy, it has been only natural to support the economy's rationalisation. Thus, a rational economy has not been a goal in and of itself any more than rationalisation has been ... but rather a means [for carrying out the party programme's goals]. Concurrently with the increase in total material welfare, the debate within Social Democracy and the trade union movement about welfare's different qualitative aspects – equality, security, different environmental assets – has been more and more intense ... Therefore, it is impossible to maintain that the party and the government disregarded the basic social democratic objectives.[11]

But it was precisely as a means for achieving security that growth was so necessary.

Thus, social democratic rhetoric bounced back and forth between on the one hand, the discussion of growth's social goals, the welfare concept and the discussion of social welfare's structure-influencing role and, on the other, this emphasis on a more rapid pace for growth. The obvious discrepancy between these two lines of thought was what resulted in protests at the party conference. As the party leadership now made clear that growth had to be the ideological priority, the party's debate on the need for increased security as a way of dealing with growth's consequences now became arguments *in favour of* growth. The discussion on exclusion as a consequence of the earlier, post-war growth policy was eliminated via references to the economic 'realities' to which social democratic ideology and policy must now adapt. The continued creation of security depended on the adaptation to economic forces that were far beyond the control of the SAP.

Productive and unproductive resources

Whereas much of the 1970s ideology broke with articulations of the post-war period and the ideology of the strong society, the party's economic discourse thus held on to the need for growth and rationalisation. Growth was again strengthened as an ideological objective, with references to its role for the creation of security. But within this social democratic worldview, security no longer played a role for growth. To that extent, there was a fundamental break with the ideology of the strong society. The 1970s saw a new economic language emerge around social policy in social democratic ideology, a language that broke with the strong society's rejection of the distinctions between production and consumption and that drew up clear boundaries between the different roles of production and consumption in the economy. Ideas of social balance and public good were downplayed. Instead, there was an acceptance of the idea that policies aiming at groups outside the labour market were essentially questions of redistribution; costs, and not investments. This also took the form of a discursive separation of functions between the public and the private sector. The Labour movement's economic discourse now seemed to accept that the private sector was driving productivity, whereas the public was not. There was an embryo here of a new idea of the role of the market for national productivity. In party economic discourse, the terms *konkurrensutsatt* (exposed to competition) and *skyddad* (sheltered from competition) were now markers of the crucial difference between public and private in the process of wealth creation. Thus, in social democratic economic policy, there was a growing split between public and private, where the public sector was increasingly articulated as an unproductive operation that laid claim to resources, whose alternative use within industry was more productive.[12]

Despite this large-scale expansion of social services, social democracy's increased ambitions in social policy of the 1970s had a circumscribed place in the discussion on growth. Rather there was a persistent stress on the transfer of resources from productive to less productive, something that in the new economic realities was increasingly problematic. The fulfilment of the social needs that had been identified in the period from the late 1960s did not, therefore, constitute productive expansion, but social policy, in the Labour movement's economic discourse, was about the transfer of resources to the unproductive groups that now constituted the costs for care and welfare. The emphasis on creating social efficiency, welfare, and freeing human resources from capitalist structures that existed in social democracy's discussions of social policy's structural or socialist role, gradually disappeared from social democratic articulations. This framing of social policy was replaced by a framing in which the demands for more resources to social policy competed with industry's need for investment within a narrowing economic scope. Ultimately, this found expression in social democratic ideology in moves to prioritise industrial investments over social reforms, and, within the emerging investment politics, in a growing emphasis on the need to transfer resources from the public sector to industry.[13] The 1972 report stated that 'capital is required for industrial investments if industry production and exports are to increase so that room can be made for resources for a progressive reform policy'.[14]

Within this new social democratic economic language of priorities, transfers, and industry, there was also a growing debate on the need to increase efficiency in the public sector, in order to free up resources for capital investment in the export sector. The 1968 economic report suggested that the public sector's operations be made more efficient 'as quickly as possible' so that resources could be transferred to the export sector.[15] A more efficient use of resources would also make it possible to make room for rising socio-political ambitions within shrinking public finances. In this way, the economic discourse of the Labour movement gradually accepted the idea, first of all, that the public sector competed with the private sector over resources, which stands in some contrast to the post-war emphasis on the role of the public sector to free up resources for the private sector. Secondly, this meant a gradual acceptance of the idea that the public sector could be made more efficient. This led to a certain conceptual slippage in social democracy's idea of efficiency. Understandings of efficiency gradually left the post-war period's emphasis on the public sector as a prerequisite for overall efficiency – *samhällsekonomisk effektivitet* or social efficiency – a concept of efficiency that was directly concerned, as we have seen, with social balance, public good, and those needs whose fulfilment was essential for social progress, and the concept of efficiency came to address a more narrow idea of efficiency as a question of strict relationship between input and output.[16]

This appears to be a break with the post-war, social democratic legacy of ideas regarding productive social policy and the strong society's view of the economic effects of public production. However, there was no direct discussion of this altered approach to social policy within social democracy. This was a shift that went somewhat unnoticed behind the intensely ideological discussion on growth's social price and the welfare concept. Moreover, the party was busy trying to face up to a growing liberal and conservative critique of the public sector and its cost, that in a sense contained framings that were rather similar to the worldview that was slowly emerging in the economic debate of the Labour movement. Social democracy dismissed this right-wing critique as building on false dichotomy between a sector that was productive and one that was unproductive, one that was competitive and one that was protected from market competition. In the 1970s political debates, the Labour movement argued that such a dichotomy disregarded the central tenets of the Swedish mixed economy and the underlying socio-economic theory of the Swedish welfare state, which was the interplay between business and an efficient public sector. The public sector, the Labour movement argued, was the prerequisite for economic efficiency and the foundation of business productivity. If no investments had been made in social services, redistribution and social policy, which consumption standard would the country have had as a foundation for stable industrial production? However, the Labour movement recognised that this interplay also meant that social democracy had to vigorously devote itself to economic productivity, since it was a prerequisite for the public sector.[17] Thus, on the surface of things, the party seemed to be defending its traditional articulations, but behind the scenes of party debates, fragments of what seemed like a radically different worldview were slowly being put in place.

Few people seem to have noticed the transition in social democracy's economic language and the gradual demise in party ideology of the idea that security had a strategic role for growth. Perhaps there didn't seem to be much to debate – the party was after all carrying out an impressive process of reform, most noticeably in childcare. There were however a few concerned voices. One such protest came in a highly ambiguous statement from Mats Hellström, member of the party executive and one of the more radical members of the Equality Group, in the discussion at the 1972 conference. Hellström saw himself forced to remind those in attendance of social democracy's view of social policy as productive policy and not as a burden on other productive activities:

> Increasingly, we [are having] a discussion in which people say that social reforms are using up our productive resources ... This should not be allowed to happen. In the same way [as in the 1920s and 1930s] ... one can claim that society's social reform policy on the eve of the 1970s does not need to be a continually greater burden for productive resources, but rather a dynamic force that can contribute to helping us out of the relative stagnation that is otherwise threatening us ... A decisive point where there must be change is the view that industrial production must pay for what society designs in the way of new public services for its citizens. The underlying mistake is precisely that some people view industrial policy and social policy as being separate and that the costs of one defray the cost of the other ... A society's industrial future depends on the problems that society takes upon itself to solve, and a society that clearly prioritises social goals can and should allow the social issues in question to also penetrate with its economic policy and its concentration on investments and technological research ... The pursuit of a socially ambitious policy today in the daily reform work for children, retirees, families with children, the physically handicapped and those excluded from society, also creates the demand and stimulus for technological development that can gradually give us increased economic room for manoeuvre. In this way, social reforms not only increase imports and decrease the balance of payments in the short term, as it is often said, but they may also be able to create the conditions necessary for industrial export and an increased flow of foreign currency in the future. Then the social reform policy can continue to be strengthened and the public sector can also expand during tougher economic times.[18]

Like industry, social policy also created demand, promoted exports and drove technology. As was the case in the 1930s, the 1970s social ambitions were also a driving force for growth.

It is unclear in Hellström's likening of the situation of the 1970s with that of the 1930s, who his target really is. His statement originated in a party debate of the Swedish right. However, his words also seem to be directed against the economic discourse of the Labour movement itself. In his comparison of the 1970s framings and those of the period between the wars, he pointed out that social policy and economic policy now opposed each other in party discourse, and that even within social democracy, there was now an economic discussion that was inconsistent with the party's traditional view of social reforms as productive politics. Hellström's intervention also echoes a concern within the Equality Group, which at this point was clearly aware of the increased stress on growth and productivity in the Economic Policy Committee, and who were strategically aware of the need to navigate the need for priorities in their proposals of reform.

When Alva Myrdal delivered the report from the Equality Group, she was clearly conscious of this point; she stressed that the group, against the background of the difficult economic situation, had chosen to recommend reforms that would 'create resources' and not 'demand resources':

> In a period when the economic situation sets rather narrow limits for new reforms, we felt it was appropriate to direct attention to just these groups because these reforms will create resources immediately. They intend to make use of heretofore untapped human resources.[19]

Groups outside the labour market – the socially maladjusted and physically handicapped, the excluded – constituted 'heretofore untapped human resources'. Therefore, the group's recommendations constituted reforms that could also be implemented during times of resource shortages.

The statements of both Hellström and Myrdal were a reminder to the party of an older rhetoric regarding the productive effects of social policy. However, in the 1970s discussion, these suggestive statements stood in stark contrast to the economic discussion regarding the transfer of resources from costs within the public sector to growth-creating investments in the economy. Social policy was no longer considered a prerequisite for growth but rather a cost for the 'productive resources'. It is in the awareness of this outlook that Alva Myrdal polemicised about the concepts of 'resource-demanding' and 'resource-creating', in the same way that, during the 1930s crisis, her husband Gunnar Myrdal had polemicised over the metaphors of 'cost' and 'investment' in the debate of social policy.

Social needs and economic expansion

This gradual slippage in the meaning of central metaphors in party economic discourse, and the outlook on socio-political expansion as a cost that must be supported by increased economic productivity, that was rejected when it came from the right, remained in economic discourse, even as the Labour movement embarked on the experiment with more radical Keynesian deficit spending in the acute economic crisis of the mid-1970s.

The collapse of the Bretton Woods system and the oil crises led in Sweden to the creation of what came to be known as the 'bridge-over policy'. The 1973 parliamentary election led to an equal distribution of seats among the party blocs, and the bridge-over policy was designed in an agreement between the social democratic government and the liberal bloc in an effort to deal with falling industrial production, increased inflation and unemployment.[20]

As its name suggests, the bridge-over policy was an attempt to 'bridge' the 1970s downturn in the world economy and protect Swedish welfare arrangements through the use of deficit spending. The bridge-over policy has been described as an in-depth Keynesian experiment, which broke with the rather moderate form of Keynesianism of the Swedish model. The crisis policy grew out of an interpretation of the oil crisis as a deep but temporary economic crisis. The overarching goal was to sustain employment. The crisis policy resulted in a highly expansive financial policy in the coming years, with considerable investments in the shipbuilding and steel industries, as well as a large-scale expansion of the public sector to create jobs and keep employment up.[21]

Within the framing of the bridge-over policy, the 1970s social democratic ambitions towards groups within social services were motivated economically, by their effects on employment. The social needs that existed in elderly care, childcare, and social services were now motivated in a series of economic reports that weighed in on the sides of both growth and security. The public sector's expansion would meet social needs, create employment opportunities, and return economic stability.[22]

However, this emphasis on the growth-promoting role of social needs was still construed around the separation of public and private in the new language of prioritisation and transfer from productive to non-productive resources. The 1975 report entitled *En demokratisk hushållning* (*Democratic economic planning*) stated that the social needs 'cost resources'. In passing, the report pointed out that while these costs were obviously 'used in production', for example, in the form of costs for welfare and care, they must be financed through increased economic productivity.[23] In spite of everything, it was still the productivity of industry that made welfare and care possible, even if it also brought about exclusion.[24]

Measuring costs: from social efficiency to cost efficiency

Beginning in the late 1960s and the early 1970s, there was an increased interest in public administration and planning, in Sweden as well as in other welfare states, with more sophisticated planning models for the monitoring and evaluation of public expenditure.

In Sweden, the analytical concepts and metaphors that emerged in the critique of the late 1960s debate on social exclusion became integrated elements in policymaking and planning in the 1970s. The problems with new and unforeseen social problems led to considerable investments in social research, in order to increase the capacity to follow social trends and identify new problems early on. The living standard measure that had been developed by the Committee on Low Income, and the concept of welfare, emerged as planning measures for social reform.[25] In the late 1960s and early 1970s, these were introduced as measures for the monitoring of social exclusion and negative effects, or costs, of growth, and social research focused on how to create a bigger balance between economic and social planning objectives and create social efficiency. However, with the 1970s experience of limited resources, the problem in the focus of policymaking was no longer how to measure social costs for growth, but how to measure the galloping costs of social security and public spending. The measures and concepts that were concerned with welfare and social efficiency in the late 1960s were now applied to measuring the efficiency of public spending.

In the LO economists' 1971 discussion, the living standard measure was put forth as a way of measuring productivity in the public sector, by focusing on social effects of public sector provisions. The concept was essential to the late

1960s critique, with its broad definition of security and its opening up of the concept of welfare as a notion of social efficiency. The living standard gauge became the basis for the development of standards for measuring the quantitative changes in peoples' feelings of security and insecurity and for putting a dimension on human welfare. To the LO economists, it was also a way of escaping the knowledge problems that were inherent in economic planning, where productivity in public production could not be measured but rather had to be set at zero.[26] It was put forward as a progressive measure for monitoring and quantifying social progress and a more adequate measure of growth in terms of human fulfillment and satisfaction.

The living standard measure was a forerunner to the growing international work, for instance in the OECD, with so-called social indicators in the 1970s. It attempted to put a quantitative measure on social effects of growth. This idea of quantifying social effects was reflected in the SAP's formulating of welfare and social efficiency in the early 1970s. They were both concepts that drew on an idea of efficiency as social efficiency, a term in which allowances had to be made for the social costs of growth. The concept of welfare was introduced into Swedish planning of the 1970s in these terms, and Swedish planning experimented with alternative methods of GDP, living standard measurements, and cost–benefit analysis based on social indicators through which social effects could be quantified and posited as costs against growth's revenues.[27]

But as the economic situation deteriorated from the mid-1970s, economic planning work began to tackle the rapid cost trends in the public sector and develop planning measures that would allow for political priorities in the use of increasingly scarce resources. The main problem was no longer creating social efficiency, but cost efficiency, through the measurement of economic efficiency and the productivity of resources used in the social sector. Social indicators and living standard measurements were never taken into economic planning in the way that was intended in the late 1960s, as a correction of the concept of GDP and its inadequacy in terms of measuring productivity in the public sector. In the 1970s, rather, they became analytical tools that served to strengthen the standing of the concept of GDP. The different discussions on the scope and limitations of productivity measurements in public provisions in the immediate post-war period and in the 1970s are indicative of the change in social democratic worldviews. When the concept of GDP was introduced into Swedish planning in 1955, the administration was extremely critical of it, specifically on the grounds that it was incapable of measuring productivity and the economic effects of the public sector's production. In the 1970s, however, GDP was now considered to be perfectly adequate for discussions on public spending and central policy decisions over the resource allocation between private and public sectors. It was argued that welfare services had no market price, since they were not turned over on a market with a price mechanism; therefore, by definition, productivity in the public sector could not be measured but must be set to zero. The discussion on welfare, economic efficiency and the measurement of social costs was brushed aside. Possible economic effects of increased welfare could not be measured and therefore could not be incorporated into any concrete planning parameters, and falling export figures meant that it was necessary to focus on the balance of payments, which meant that adjustments in resource allocations and the scope of consumption could only consider those economic factors that were strictly quantifiable within the parameters set by GDP. This demanded that more attention be paid to matters of efficiency and productivity within the 'protected' sector.[28] Planning had to provide for measures that would allow for the public sector to be made more efficient, in order to enable the transfer of resources to industry.[29]

Based on this emphasis on 'greater efficiency', economic planning began to focus on developing methods for resource evaluations and productivity measurements in social enterprises. The previous work on social research and living standard measurements now became the knowledge basis for planning models that focused on the evaluation of the cost-benefit of social policy, in order to provide for political priorities in the use of limited resources. This interest in the efficiency of public spending quickly developed from an emphasis on rationalisation interest in order to allow for increased social ambitions in a shrinking economic space, to straightforward discussions on cost-cutting and saving in order to shift resources from the public sector to the export industry. When the government created the Institute for Social Research in 1972 under the leadership of Sten Johansson, the same Sten Johansson who had developed the living standard measure together with Per Holmberg, an explicit motivation was to increase control over the costs put into social policy in order to increase knowledge of possible areas of rationalisation and saving in public sector expenditure.[30]

The working group behind the Institute for Social Research was of the opinion that social research had not concentrated sufficiently on the relationship between invested economic resources and the effects of socio-political reforms. Like research on business economics, social research should focus on producing evaluation methods that could quantify and measure social policy's effects, as well as their 'return'.[31]

> The rapid cost development within the socio-political sector, combined with raised social ambitions, has led to demands for a better prioritisation of social investments, including the desire for some type of cost–benefit analysis of different socio-political measures and investments ... However, it will likely be difficult to quantify social policy's 'return' in monetary terms, which is required if one is to apply the cost–benefit method immediately ... Accordingly, research on how cost–benefit analysis can be applied to socio-political measures is required as a foundation for prioritisation within the socio-political area. As a complement to using other scientific methods as a starting point, we must design models for evaluating social investments. The Committee on Low Income has provided interesting examples on this method of attacking a problem.[32]

Via formulations such as 'evaluation', 'more efficient prioritisation' and 'cost development', it became clear that it was not social aspects of economic development that were at the centre of the research but rather the costs of social policy.[33] The living standard concept was now seen as a tool for creating quantitative foundations for measuring social effects and, in this way, for evaluating the economic resources being used in social policy. Cost–benefit analyses would be used to measure cost efficiency and the value of invested resources, not questions of social efficiency or the functioning of the economy as a whole.

In the late 1960s, there were also attempts to strengthen the role of the budget as a tool for long-term planning, in order to increase the political control of the use of resources in the public sector and increase budget flexibility in order to deal more quickly with changes in the economic climate. As part of this process, Swedish eyes turned to the US and the work that had been done there with so-called programme budgeting or PPB.[34]

Programme budgeting was developed within the United States Department of Defense in the 1960s, in order to strengthen control over the defence budget. Programme budgeting meant that the budget would be increasingly used as a means of control. By dividing the budget into a programme with clearly formulated goals, it would be possible to weigh and evaluate resource use against goal fulfilment, costs against achievements. The methods developed for the defence industry were later applied to the American War on Poverty under the Johnson administration.[35] In Sweden, the interest in programme budgeting stemmed back to the observation, from the mid 1950s, that it was very hard to measure productivity and efficiency in the public sector within the parameters of the GDP concept. As the concept of GDP was introduced into a sceptical Swedish administration, concessions were made to develop measures better equipped to deal with the public sector that had such a central role in the Swedish economy. PPB first became interesting to Swedish policymakers from this perspective, and the Swedish administration followed the American work with PPB from early on in the 1960s.

The interest in PPB shifted decisively, however, from the 1950s to the 1970s. From within the worldview of the strong society, PPB was seen as a possible tool for increasing the efficiency of public sector production, something that in light of the huge resources put into public sector expansion was considered to be of central importance for national efficiency. The interpretation of efficiency, though, and the purpose of budget evaluation, in the early 1960s, was that it would lead to a better understanding of the social need gratification that occurred in public production and thereby to better understandings of social balance and the role of public good in the Swedish economy.[36] The idea that PPB could be used to measure cost efficiency was explicitly rejected. Cost efficiency was far too narrow a concept when productivity and efficiency in the public sector were measured, since this was a matter of public good and social balance.[37] When PPB was introduced in the process of budget reform beginning in the late 1960s, there was a lengthy discussion of the need for a concept of economic efficiency that would take into account social need gratification and qualitative factors as the foundation for budget decisions. These considerations were said to be indispensable for social investments and other factors that were particularly vital, such as the effects of social reforms or investments in the public sector that could not be measured or evaluated in monetary terms. Living standard components and social indicators were identified as one way of accurately defining goals in a programme budgeting system; they made it possible to create clearer measures of efficiency for factors that were difficult to quantify, as well as to measure economic effects. However, because the use of these components as the foundation for planning was still linked to considerable methodological difficulties, much more development work was required. For this reason, the Budget Commission kept to a narrower productivity concept, one that focused on cost effectiveness and rejected more general notions of social efficiency.[38] Cost efficiency would form the basis for political decisions on resource allocation in the budget. It was exactly such a narrow definition of productivity and efficiency that had been rejected in the early 1960s. When it was finally introduced into Swedish planning, programme budgeting thus became a tool for controlling the cost efficiency of public resources, with the purpose of transferring resources to industry, and questions of social need gratification, social efficiency or indeed of welfare disappeared.

Swedosclerosis and faith in the future

The idea of the cost efficiency of the public sector as the 1970s' biggest problem and increased efficiency and rationalisation as the way forward grew in importance in the 1970s debate on growing budget deficits. The public sector and its costs were now viewed as the economy's real problem child, in Sweden as well as in the surrounding world.

In 1977, a group of experts in the OECD published the McCracken report, which maintained that the biggest problems of the 1970s were the enormous cost increases and the expansionary policies pursued on the heels of the decade's increased social demands.[39] In 1976, the SAP had lost the parliamentary election to a liberal coalition, and the report had an immediate impact on the Liberal government under the leadership of the Center party's Torbjörn Fälldin. In its wake, the Fälldin government appointed an economic delegation in 1978 to discuss the relationship between growth and the welfare state in the Swedish economy. In its report the following year, the Commission asserted that the public sector's expansion, an excessively high tax burden and a social safety net that undermined the labour market's incentive structure, were driving up Swedish costs and forcing the country's export industry out of the international marketplace. Under social democratic policy, the constantly growing social demands of the electorate had been met by the continuous expansion of public consumption. The Commission concluded that new forms for public production, greater efficiency, the introduction of fees in welfare services and semi-privatisations must be considered.[40]

This discussion echoed the rising intellectual currents of monetarism, public choice theory, and neo-liberalism, that were to come to the fore in the coming decade. Social democracy criticised the Liberal government's economic policy in a series of economic reports and parliamentary bills that stressed the interplays between the welfare state and the historical growth rates of the Swedish economy. It maintained that there was a strong link between public sector consumption and economic production, and between growth and social goals. Mats Hellström's words from the 1972 party congress, where they seemed to incorporate a critique of the party's own economic discourse, reverberated in this critique, now directed at the Swedish right:

> A society's industrial future is dependent on the problems that society undertakes to solve, and a society that gives strong precedence to social goals can and should allow social issues to penetrate its economic policy.[41]

While social democracy in this way criticised the economic policies of the Liberal government, it was clear that its own economic discourse was beginning to change. In 1977 the former Minister of Finance under Erlander, Gunnar Sträng, celebrated his 80th birthday. At a party seminar held in conjunction with Sträng's birthday, a new generation of party thinkers, amongst them the future Minister of Finance Kjell-Olof Feldt, debated new courses for economic policy and the need for combating inflation, recreating stability, and increasing savings in the Swedish economy. In the preface to the published pamphlet, Olof Palme likened this emerging new economic strategy with social democracy's successful formulation of an economic strategy in the 1930s Depression. Just as the party's 'new economic ideas' in the 1930s had been based on 'a belief in the rational' (*förnuftstro*) on the part of the progressive economic thinkers of the era, such as Ernst Wigforss and Nils Karleby, so must the party now place its faith in a new generation of social democratic-minded economists, instead of falling for the utopias of the late 1960s behavioural scientists and ecologists, 'salvation prophets and charlatans'. With this belief in the rational, social democracy would arrive at progressive solutions to the new economic problems and recreate a belief in the future (*framtidstro*) of Swedish politics.[42]

Concluding remarks

The developments in 1970s ideology were deeply contradictory. Beneath the grandeur of the SAP's discussion of individual welfare and security as the guiding stars of the Labour movement's 1970s policies and the expansion of social rights that this meant in a wide range of areas, it is possible to see a gradually emerging language around welfare reform that was distinct from the SAP's historic articulations. This language focused on the separation between productive and non-productive elements in the economy. Where 1930s discourse emphasised the links between the activities for the reproduction of labour taking place in the public sector and production in industry, 1970s economic discourse gave a clear priority to the latter. The public sector was consumption, not production, and in a world of shrinking resources, production had to come first. This same dichotomy was applied to the social sphere. Where 1930s functional socialism set in place a worldview that stressed the interdependencies between work and need over the life cycle, 1970s social democratic ideology spoke of the productive and the unproductive as two fundamentally different groups in society, where one was a burden on the other.

The notion of 'cost' came to incorporate a significant opening in this process of rearticulation. The late 1960s formulation of 'cost' as the social cost for growth and production, was replaced in the course of the 1970s by a notion of 'cost' that identified the costs of social policy as costs that must be paid for with more production and growth.

Notes

1 SAP 1975a.
2 Benner 1997 p. 113f.
3 Pontusson 1992.
4 SAP 1968; SAP 1967 conference protocol p. 186.
5 SAP 1968 p. 13.
6 LO-SAP 1972, *Näringspolitisk rapport* p. 106f.
7 Ibid p. 18; SAP 1972 conference protocol p. 452f.
8 SAP 1972 C 31–54.
9 SAP 1972 conference protocol pp. 452, 459.
10 SAP 1972 conference protocol p. 185.
11 Ibid.
12 This division also defined the EFO-model for wage determination; see Ryner p. 135.
13 SAP 1972 conference protocol p. 185.
14 LO-SAP 1972 pp. 19, 107.
15 SAP 1968 p. 47.
16 Ibid p. 48.
17 SAP 1972 conference protocol p. 466.
18 SAP 1972 conference protocol pp. 500–502.
19 SAP 1972 conference protocol pp. 153; SAP 1972a p. 15.
20 Jonung, L., 1999, *Med backspegeln som kompass*, DS 1999:9, Stockholm, p. 163f.
21 Benner 1997 p. 142f; Jonung 1999 p. 163f.
22 SAP 1975a p. 95; LO-SAP 1973, *Sysselsättningspolitik för 1970–talet*; LO-SAP 1978, *Sysselsättningspolitik för 1980–talet;* SAP 1979, *En social näringspolitik;* SOU 1975: 89, p. 17; SOU 1978:14; SOU 1975:90.
23 SAP 1975a p. 95.
24 SAP 1975a p. 101; LO-SAP 1978; SAP 1979.
25 Ayres 1998 p. 104; Arndt 1989 p. 89.
26 Burstedt 1971; LO 1971; OECD 1971.
27 Ds U 1971:4 s. 60–98; Ds S 1970:2 s. 421f.; Johansson 1979 p. 6f.
28 SOU 1970:71 pp. 19, 48.
29 SOU 1970:71 pp. 19, 48; SOU 1975:89 pp. 23, 27.
30 Forskningsberedningen (Council of science) 1968; Ds S 1973:1; Ds S 1973:8 pp. 6, 16, 21.
31 Ds U 1971:4 pp. 33–34.
32 Ds U 1971:4 p. 69.
33 Ds U 1971:4 p. 69.
34 Ministry of Finance, 1969, *Programbudgetering.*

35 O'Connor 2000 p. 174; Haveman, R., 1987, *Poverty policy and poverty research, the great society and the social sciences*, University of Wisconsin Press, Madison.
36 SOU 1967:11 p. 11f; 1967:13 pp. 9–11.
37 SOU 1967:11 pp. 15–17. SOU 1973:43 p. 38.
38 SOU 1973:43 pp. 20, 52, 59f.
39 OECD 1977 pp. 17, 37.
40 Ds Ju 1979:1 pp. 10, 23, 34, 36, 89–117; Ds Ju 1979:2; Benner 1997 pp. 130–145.
41 LO-SAP 1978 p. 34; SAP 1979.
42 SAP 1977, *Ekonomisk politik inför 1980–talet*, p. 13.

6

Can we afford security? Social policy in the third way

Introduction

Olof Palme's 1970s idea of a third way in a new and more social concept of growth gave way to a new idea of a third way in the early 1980s. This 1980s third way was a different utopia. It was deeply concerned with growth, but less so with its social content. It made a decisive break with the late 1960s radicalism. However, it also broke with a lot of social democracy's historical articulations around the welfare state. To social democratic values of security and solidarity as the route to individual emancipation, it added market efficiency.

In the previous chapter, the changes in the discourse surrounding social policy in the 1970s were considered as a gradual elimination of the party's radical articulations of social exclusion, welfare, and social efficiency, and the emergence of articulations that focused on questions of cost efficiency and on transferring resources from the public sector to Swedish industry. What is striking about these shifts and slippages in the 1970s is that they largely occurred silently, through a progressive shift in economic metaphors and concepts in politics and planning, and that they also happened parallel to the party's radicalisation in many social issues without causing too much controversy. However, in the period beginning with the end of the 1970s, these silent shifts culminated in a heated discursive struggle, as the SAP was faced with critique both from a mobilising Swedish right and with new articulations that came from emerging groups within the Labour movement. The tensions and vacillations that were deep in 1970s ideology now surfaced, in a party debate that concerned overriding ideological goals and the relationship between growth and security in party ideology.

The collapse of the Bretton Woods system after the oil crises that followed the revolution in Iran, and the problems with large scale unemployment, growing budget deficits and inflation in the industrialised West, led to a reinterpretation of the 1970s crisis in Western societies, from interpretations of it as a cyclical downturn that could be handled through Keynesian demand management in order to protect welfare state arrangements, to interpretations of a thoroughgoing structural crisis that challenged those very institutions. An increasingly ideological neo-liberal critique targeted the welfare state and identified the expansion of public expenditure as a key factor behind the economic crisis.[1]

In the United Kingdom and USA, under the governments of Margaret Thatcher and Ronald Reagan respectively, economic policy shifted towards restraint, with major cuts in social spending. In Chile, Augusto Pinochet's junta began to experiment with radical market liberalisation.[2] Influenced by the ideas of Milton Friedman and Friedrich von Hayek, translated into Swedish and published in the late 1970s by the right-wing publishing house Timbro, an increasingly radicalised Swedish right, headed by the SAF (the Swedish Employers' Federation), also began a crusade against the social democratic welfare state.[3] Swedish political language in the 1980s went through a significant escalation. Right-wing discourse focused on Olof Palme, who also stepped up his rhetoric.[4] In a famous speech to the metal workers' (*Metallarbetareförbundet*) congress in 1981, Palme likened the Swedish employers to the Chilean junta and described neo-liberal ideology as the 'happy marriage of military dictatorship and the free market'. Sweden, Palme said, would never be Friedman's and Pinochet's Chile, nor would it Thatcher's Britain.[5]

A lot of the Swedish debate focused on the public sector and on the need for cuts and savings in public expenditure.[6] In 1980, the liberal government proposed a programme of austerity, with cuts in the public sector, and in the following year a committee of enquiry, the Expert Group for Study of the Public Sector (*Expertgruppen för studier i offentlig ekonomi*), ESO, was appointed to develop measures of the productivity of the public sector: measures that could provide a basis for strategic budget decisions and savings within social policy.[7] During the late 1970s and early 1980s, the Social Democratic party went on the attack against this critique. The Liberal government's crisis policy was depicted as a bourgeois plot to first destroy public finances and create a narrative of crisis, and then dismantle the welfare state (*social nedrustning*).[8] The writings of Milton Friedman and Friedrich von Hayek were dismissed as 'bourgeois propaganda' and new expressions of the same right-wing critique of the costs of the welfare state that the Social Democrats had been contending with since the breakthrough of Keynesian policies in the 1930s. During the election campaigns before the parliamentary elections of 1979 and 1982, the SAP countered Friedman and von Hayek with the classical formulations in defence of public consumption of Ernst Wigforss, the main thinker of the 1930s.[9]

Up until the second lost election of 1979, the Labour movement maintained its 1970s social ambitions, with its offensive against social exclusion, its promises of continued investment for vulnerable groups and calls for a further expansion of the public sector. When the Liberal government enacted the Social Welfare Act in 1982, the Social Democrats protested against how the new legislation was not given any financial resources. 'Sweden can afford social security!' was the slogan on Labour Day hoardings before the election in 1982, as the

Labour movement protested against the government's plan to introduce an extra qualification day for health insurance entitlements.[10]

But while Olof Palme and Ingvar Carlsson defended the economic theory of the welfare state in the electoral campaigns, the critique grew within the ranks of the social democratic movement and a change of ideological course gradually also took form within the SAP. The lost election in 1979 led to a process of rearticulation, which culminated in the crisis programme that formed the basis for the social democratic strategy in the 1982 election. The Social Democrats were returned to power in 1982 with a manifesto that paved a third way out of crisis, a manifesto in which saving and cost-cutting were cornerstones of a social democratic strategy of reform.

The introduction of the third way in the Crisis Programme has been described as a dramatic break with the post-war period – a wind shift to the right – in which social democracy adopted the language and the framings of neo-liberalism and the Swedish right.[11] But the language of the Crisis Programme emanated in a group of social democratic modernisers who, not unlike the way in which social workers and LO economists in the late 1960s had challenged the party over discrepancies between party ideology and social reality, put forward conceptions of a dramatically altered economic reality that required ideological adaptation. Similarly to how '1968' in the Swedish context took the form of a radical left *within* social democracy, advocating ideological change after what they saw as a new social reality, this 'neo-liberal' critique of the 1980s was also a radical social democracy of sorts, advocating renewal in order to create a better fit between social democratic ideology and a dramatically different economic world.

Knowledge for the future – the Social Democratic Economists

In 1979 a discussion group known as the Social Democratic Economists (*Socialdemokratiska ekonomgruppen*), the SDE, was formed. This group consisted of a circle of active social democratic economists from the trade union movement and the Stockholm School of Economics.[12] The group was formed as a reaction to the Social Democrats' defeat in the 1979 election and to affirm the party's hope of regaining parliamentary power. The defeat was interpreted as the outcome of the party's failure to formulate a credible alternative to the austerity policies of the Liberal government. The SDE contrasted the SAP's traditional defence of the public sector and its pursuit of more ambitious social policies with a reality of *crisis*, a radically different economic world that required a fundamental rethinking of major elements of post-war social democratic ideology. Influenced by the so-called 'new economic ideas', they argued that the post-war ideology and the party's economic policies were outdated, outrun by the changes in the international economy and no longer able to provide a coherent defence of social democratic values.

In the early years of the 1980s, these SDE economists, with their special insights into economic reality, claimed to possess authoritative knowledge of the central economic policy problem and the ways in which social democratic ideology had to be modified in order to address it. The members of the group saw their task as one of providing points of departure for an ideological renewal based on their economic expertise, as well as on their standing as professional economists and active Social Democrats. Indeed, their mission was 'to liberate the party from traditionalist economic thinking' and to create a social democratic economic policy that could act as a counterbalance to the growing criticism from the right. In the opinion of the group, the effective defence of social democratic values required that social democracy take serious account of the content of this right-wing critique and of the new economic ideas on which it was based.[13]

In a 1981 memorandum the SDE claimed that a central ideological task was to review the 'new economic ideas', in order to

> distinguish between serious economic analysis and crude right-wing propaganda, and determine which points we have to repudiate on ideological grounds and which ones contain ideas that could be applied in social democratic policy as well ...[14]

The phrase 'new economic ideas' was an obvious play of words, referring to the influence of Keynesian ideas and the Stockholm School in the crisis policies of the SAP in the 1930s. During the autumn of 1981, the group arranged for case studies to be made of economic policy changes in the USA, the United Kingdom and Chile.[15]

The public sector stood at the centre of the need for ideological rearticulation. Defending the public sector against the critique from the right, along with maintaining it and reforming it as an ideological legacy, was considered a central task for the group, both 'as Social Democrats and economists'.[16]

> The public sector lacks the features that we would like to endow it with, based on our socialist premises.[17]

At a meeting in June 1980, the SDE decided to undertake a special study of the concept of efficiency and attempt to answer the following question: How should modern social democracy's concept of efficiency differ from the one on which the expansion of the public sector in the 1950s, 1960s and 1970s had been based?

> What goals and what view of efficiency in the public administration will characterise Social Democracy during the 1980s? How do these objectives differ from those that prevailed during the 60s and 70s?[18]

Was it possible, for instance, to systematically compare productivity in the public sector with productivity in industry, which had been the guiding star of the investigations into public policy carried out by the ESO under the Liberal government?[19] In other words, the group placed the concept of efficiency at the centre of the process of ideological renewal and at the heart of future social policy reform projects. However, the question of the correct interpretation of the concept of efficiency as applied to the public sector gave rise to deep divisions within the group.[20] In fact, the SDE was a group that incorporated two radically different worldviews. One, represented by the trade union economists in the group, sternly defended the 'old' ideology and the historical outlook of the SAP on public sector provisions and social services as productive and means for growth. The other, represented by the group of younger economists led by Klas Eklund, later the director of the Swedish central bank, called for ideological renewal, and advocated saving and cost-cutting as the radical means of reform. The meetings of the group consequently became the arena of a discursive struggle that took the form of a clash between old and new, over the correct interpretation of crisis and the role of the public sector in creating it. The central metaphor underpinning the critique of the latter, rapidly gaining in influence, was 'efficiency'. But efficiency was given a meaning radically different from its 1970s connotations to welfare and the minimisation of social costs. Efficiency was not 'social efficiency' (*samhällsekonomisk effektivitet*) but 'cost efficiency' (*kostnadseffektivitet*).

In November 1980, the SDE arranged a seminar on the efficiency of the public sector. This began as a defence of the public sector and the welfare state. The public sector was not the problem of the Swedish economy. The services produced in the public sector were instead a prerequisite for industrial productivity and for continued growth. However, behind this rhetorical defence, the seminar focused strongly on the role of the public sector in the economic crisis.[21]

At the seminar, Klas Eklund, then an economist at the Stockholm School of Economics, claimed that the expansion of the public sector had caused the increase in the budget deficit and galloping inflation. In Eklund's opinion, this situation required a fundamental re-evaluation of social democracy's approach to the public sector.

> Our conclusion is therefore disturbingly clear. There is no possibility of expanding the public sector in the 1980s ... However, we are not saying that we should reduce the size of the public sector, but rather that its growth must quite obviously be restrained ... In addition, we have concluded that one of today's pre-eminent tasks is to improve the efficiency of the public sector, and in so doing maintain and even improve the services provided to the public, even if the expansion rate had to be decelerated. Finally, it is particularly important that a debate on how to deal with these tasks in accordance with our underlying objectives on the redistribution of wealth and our attitudes to solidarity get under way immediately.[22]

According to Eklund, greater and increased efficiency was imperative in a time of crisis, both in order to reduce the budget deficit and to maintain the party's ideological aspirations. He issued a decisive warning against interpreting discussions about improved efficiency as right-wing scaremongering. Greater efficiency and cuts in expenditure were not *per se* ideologically negative, as they need not necessarily affect the most vulnerable groups. Indeed, improving efficiency was one route to ideological renewal of the public sector, and a core means of safeguarding security in a period of crisis.[23] Support for this standpoint came in a contribution from the sociologist Sten Johansson, whose radical work with social exclusion, low wages and social indicators has been discussed earlier. Johansson pointed to the ongoing work with social indicators. However, his idea of the political application of social indicators had changed. Whereas in the 1960s Johansson saw them as a critical tool for assessing the *social* impact of social reform, he now argued that social indicators should be used to evaluate efficiency in social spending and provide the basis for making decisions regarding necessary cuts. Which measures had the greatest significance for vulnerable groups and in which programmes could efficiency be improved? 'In the economic situation we are facing, we cannot afford to get things wrong.'[24]

In this discussion, efficiency became a powerful metaphor for framing a particular problem, namely, the cost of security and the inefficiency of the public sector. It was precisely this formulation of the problem that social democracy had opposed when it was expressed by the Swedish right. As a problem-generating metaphor, 'efficiency' stands in interesting contrast to the way 'social exclusion' became a metaphor for the social costs of growth as it was put forward by the social workers and trade union economists in the late 1960s. Not only did 'efficiency' convey the persuasive message of the excessive costs for social security; it also contained a clear idea of the direction of problem-solving: cutting the costs of the public sector. In this respect, it embodied a completely different idea of efficiency from the ideas of a socially sustainable capitalism that had been advocated in the late 1960s.

This reconceptualisation of efficiency from 'social efficiency' to 'cost efficiency' did not go unnoticed. Protests were lodged against a social democratic understanding of efficiency as a question of cost effectiveness and rationalisation. The seminar was attended by two economists from the Swedish Municipal Workers' Union (*Kommunalarbetareförbundet*), Bo Johansson and Jan Kolk. Their rejoinder was based on a publication from the union's conference in 1980 entitled *An overall approach to efficiency* (*En helhetssyn på effektiviteten*). Johansson and Kolk advocated a socio-economic approach to the public sector. They warned explicitly against transferring a profit-based concept of productivity from industry and private services to the production of health and social services. This was a productivity concept that they claimed brought with it 'obvious risks of political decisions being based on erroneous conclusions about productivity, with negative socio-economic consequences'.[25]

In this reading, 'efficiency' became a metaphor for the productive effects of social policy and the public sector, a metaphor that was used to defend social democracy's historical framings and the ideas of the strong society. During the late 1970s and early 1980s the trade union movement used this interpretation of 'efficiency' as social efficiency as the basis for its criticism of the measurements made of the productivity of the public sector in economic planning and what was now referred to as the 'zeroing' of its productivity. In 1980 the Council of Nordic Trade Unions, SAMAK, an umbrella organisation for the trade union movements in the Nordic countries, published a report in defence of the public sector, *The trade union movement and the public sector* (*Fackföreningsrörelsen och den offentliga sektorn*). In this report Rudolf Meidner criticised measurements of productivity in public services which, he claimed, were based on the fictitious division between 'producing' and 'consuming' sectors in neo-classical economic theory. This division, whose origins Meidner traced back to Adam Smith in *The wealth of nations,* had not become more convincing just because it was put forward by Margaret Thatcher or the Swedish Employers' Confederation a few centuries later, Meidner wrote. It was still logically flawed. In his opinion, the conception of a productive and an unproductive sector lay behind the zeroing of productivity in the public services. This statistical 'distortion of reality' meant that an expanding public sector would always display declining productivity, while at the same time it would be making an ever-growing, albeit immeasurable, contribution to increasing industrial productivity.[26]

Meidner's arguments were repeated in the 1982 report entitled *Threatened sector* (*Hotad sektor*). Like the Municipal Workers' report and Rudolf Meidner's thesis, this report demanded the inclusion of the qualitative effects of public sector production and the costs it bore on behalf of the industrial sector in a more refined concept of productivity, so that the profits from industrial production could be weighed against losses for society as a whole.[27]

Threatened sector was written as a protest against the increasingly important role played by productivity measurements in political attitudes to the public sector and the demand for savings. In 1981, Ingemar Mundebo, budget minister in the Liberal government, established the Expert Group for Study of the Public Sector, the ESO. According to its directive, the group was to provide sounder information on which to base socio-economic decisions by developing better methods for the measurement of efficiency and productivity in public sector activities. However, the ESO never measured any socio-economic effects. Rather, it concentrated narrowly on productivity, making its measurements through comparisons between the productivity of services in the public and private sectors.[28] In the studies of productivity and efficiency that the ESO made during the 1980s, a preconception about productivity can be glimpsed in the form of theoretical assumptions about the declining marginal utility of investments in public services.[29] Based on its data regarding productivity in the public sector, the ESO concluded that productivity was decreasing. Although resources allocated to the public sector had grown continually in the post-war period, it was impossible to measure any positive changes in productivity. This indicated declining dividends from invested capital. The logical conclusion from these assumptions was that productivity would continue to decline with further investment, until it finally ceased completely.[30]

It was these conclusions and their implications about which the trade union economists were warning.

The discussions of the SDE therefore took the form of a discursive struggle over knowledge, a conflict between social democracy's historical framings concerning the social impact of production in the public sector and the new framings, influenced by the 'new economic ideas', about its costliness and inefficiency. Just as the struggle over the concept of social exclusion in the 1960s had escalated to embrace overarching ideological goals and the relationship between growth and security, this struggle would also embrace fundamental ideological standpoints about the economic role of the public sector, and ultimately the relationship between growth and security in social democratic ideology.

Politics of safeguarding

The SDE's critique of the cost of the public sector prompted a process of re-articulation of social democratic ideology. In the run-up to the 1982 election, social democracy put safeguarding (*slå vakt om*) at the heart of its campaign, setting this up against a right-wing campaign for dismantling the welfare state (*systemskifte*). The content of safeguarding was that defending the welfare state in a time of economic crisis would mean a re-evaluation of the means of reform, and an opening up in social democratic ideology to allow for substantial cuts in the public sector. Safeguarding, then, required some substantial rethinking of social democratic ideology, and in this process of rearticulation the party took on board the economic ideas and metaphors put forward by the younger, modernising part of the SDE.

In 1980 the party executive established a Crisis Group under the leadership of Ingvar Carlsson, charged with thinking up a platform for a new social democratic crisis policy that would give the party a social democratic interpretation of crisis much in the same way that social democracy had embraced radically new economic ideas in the policies developed to face the 1930s Depression. The members of the SDE had a great deal of influence on the establishment of this group and the SDE's debate influenced the programme that was written to a very large extent.

The work of the Crisis Group and the manifesto it submitted to the 1981 congress, *Future for Sweden* (*Framtid för Sverige*), broke with social democracy's historic articulations.[31] The introduction to the programme stated that this was not a normal programme of reform. The situation for social democracy was essentially different from that of previous periods. Whereas post-war social democratic policy had concerned the redistribution of assets on the basis of a continually expanding economic base, now a 'sound economy' had to be recreated. This was a programme for a social democratic *crisis* policy. Therefore, the main problem for social democracy was the creation of growth.

> Today's problems illustrate with full clarity that economic growth is needed to maintain the standards we enjoy in Sweden. This is more than necessary if we are to be able to deal with the shortcomings that still exist in our community. Improving conditions for children, offering the physically challenged the same possibilities of a full, rich life as other citizens ... all of this demands great economic resources, so great that we can only procure them through increased growth in the economy.[32]

Previous criticism of growth, and the social democratic preoccupation in the 1970s with the problem of social exclusion as a consequence of growth, were now described as a 'fallacious'. The evidence for this was that all social problems had become worse during the economic crisis. In other words, the zero growth that was demanded in the late 1960s had led only to further exclusion. It was not growth itself that was the source of social exclusion; rather the problem had been the specific form that growth had taken during the post-war period.

Lessons had been learnt from these problems and, according to the programme, the earlier arguments *against* growth were therefore really arguments *for* growth. The third way policy would be devised in the interface between the need for the gains from growth and the political insight into the losses growth could incur for security.[33]

Fundamentally, creating growth in the 1980s crisis meant that social democratic policy had to be modified. No resources for enabling greater security were available.

According to the Crisis Programme, government finance faced one main problem, namely, public consumption was expanding more rapidly than production. Quite simply, Sweden was living beyond its means. For this reason, social democratic policy also had to focus on a 'reconstruction' of the Swedish economy through savings and major retrenchment in the public sector. 'Saving' therefore became a key concept in social democratic crisis policy. However, cuts in public expenditure seemed like a violation of post-war social democratic ideology and were not far removed in substance from the Liberal crisis policy that had been attacked by social democracy as an attempt to dismantle the welfare state. Thus, the programme had to convince the party of the ideological correctness of saving as a means of reform and contrast this social democratic crisis policy with the crisis policy of the right, while at the same time successfully silencing rival framings from within the Labour movement.

The Crisis Group solved this dilemma by formulating the policy it proposed as a path to security. This crisis policy, it argued, formed the basis of an 'offensive' policy that would safeguard and maintain security in the face of the Liberal government's attack on welfare, just as the 1930s crisis policy had vanquished right-wing criticism of social policy. The social democratic policy was a policy for social welfare and individual security because it was based on the values of solidarity and security, even if the methods discussed for reconstruction were easy to confuse with those advocated by the right. The differences in the values underlying the social democratic and right-wing ideas of saving were emphasised time and time again in the rhetoric surrounding the programme.[34] Accordingly, social democracy considered that security was becoming more and more important during the economic crisis. In *Future for Sweden,* this opinion was contrasted with what was portrayed as a right-wing dogma that identified insecurity as a necessary element of a crisis policy. In social democracy's view, the crisis itself created an insecurity that affected the most vulnerable and weakest groups and ultimately threatened to undermine society as a whole. Security, therefore, was a prerequisite for any effective crisis policy, since insecurity was a destructive force, incapable of creating the circumstances required for stable and efficient production. Crisis policy therefore had to be based on an equitable redistribution policy so that individuals could shoulder the burdens in solidarity; the Crisis Programme asserted that the defence of the public sector and its importance for the security of the weakest groups in the community constituted a central ideological task.[35]

However, behind this emphasis on traditional social democratic values, the programme made it clear that the crisis brought with it a change in the conditions that applied to security. The defence of security must not prevent social democracy from realising the gravity of the situation. In actual fact, now the situation was essentially different from the crisis of the 1930s. As the 1970s had demonstrated, it would be impossible to use expansionary measures (as the party had done in the 1930s) to escape the problems of the 1980s. Nor was it possible to increase austerity and further exacerbate unemployment. The solution was the 'third way' between expansion and austerity. Unlike the discussions of crisis policy in the 1930s of saving *or* working, now it was a question of saving *and* working, of cutting public sector expenditure while redirecting investment to industry to keep up employment levels.

This third way version of saving was not a form of social dismantling but rather one phase of an 'offensive' strategy. The programme compared the attitude to saving in the third way with the ideas expressed by Ernst Wigforss about saving in the 1930s crisis policy, and even brought in a quote from his famous 1932 pamphlet *Can we afford to work*? (*Ha vi råd att arbeta?*):

> Consideration for the future has always been a requirement of a sound household [*hushållning*], and therefore saving has come mainly to mean refraining from spending one's entire income on immediate, day-to-day needs and instead reserving some portion to ensure that one's livelihood will be more secure and preferably more rewarding in the future. Here we can see the true reason for saving: it is required to resolve certain problems; it is not a solution in itself. If there is to be any point to saving it must be linked to ways of using savings that will really lead to results in the form of 'more secure livelihoods'. Then saving becomes part of an offensive strategy for greater welfare, not a defensive adaptation to the deterioration of the conditions that prevail for welfare.[36]

In this way, saving was articulated as a temporary austerity measure to ensure greater wealth tomorrow. In actual fact, saving was one element in an ideological offensive for security, and not a 'defensive adaptation' to economic circumstances.[37]

There was, of course, a crucial difference between the concept of saving in *Future for Sweden* and saving in Wigforss's original pamphlet, and the Crisis Programme's reading of Wigforss was a rather blatant misrepresentation of the content of the original pamphlet. Wigforss, a member of the expansion-oriented younger Stockholm School and the Unemployment Commission, was writing polemically against the austerity measures demanded by the liberal older Stockholm School in the 1930s Depression. In fact, Wigforss's critique of the 'bourgeois concept of saving' took the form of a plea for a radical socialist expansionary economic policy centered on public works, extensive social policies and public consumption. His pamphlet, which was published before the election in 1932, the same year that Gunnar Myrdal's article on productive social policies appeared, contained powerful arguments against viewing public consumption as 'unproductive' and a 'burden on industry', and emphasised it as a central means of freeing productive capacity and recreating economic growth.[38]

This difference in the interpretation of the concept of saving came back to the difference in conceptions of the role of social policy for growth. Whereas the crisis policy of the 1930s viewed social policy as an investment in productivity, the 1980s crisis policy was based on the belief that social policy was a cost, one where savings could be made in order to transfer resources to more productive activities. The discussion of savings in *Future for Sweden* culminated in the conclusion that cuts had to be made in public consumption to enable resources to be transferred to industry.

For this reason, expenditures in the public sector required careful study. Cuts or re-evaluations had to be made of certain costs 'that, when appraised for their significance, cannot be given priority in attaining central welfare and redistribution objectives', and instead the focus had to shift to others that were vital for 'safeguarding' social security. According to the Crisis Programme, two areas were so important that they had to be allowed to continue to expand – care of the elderly and the continued expansion of childcare, which was a strategically important reform since it put women at work. Also, the party had had a huge fight with the women's groups over childcare in the 1970s and the expansion of childcare was therefore hard to back down on.[39] All other aspects of the public sector had to be re-examined. The conditions that applied to social policy in the 1980s differed fundamentally from those of the 1950s and 1960s. There were no resources for social reforms. Instead of augmenting resources, new methods now had to be found to create security.

> For Social Democracy the public sector remains an important instrument for the realisation of our political objectives. But the ways in which we use this instrument have to be different in the 1980s for the manifest reason that the problems we are tackling look different.[40]

The Crisis Programme therefore signified the articulation of a new link between growth and security, where the creation of growth required cuts in security. The distinction between productive and unproductive resources embodied in 1970s investment policies was now being given explicit formulation as part of the social democratic crisis policy. Despite the party's efforts to reconcile them, once again growth and security were ultimately expressed as deeply antagonistic objectives in social democratic ideology.

However, the gradual ideological changes that had attracted relatively little attention in the 1970s now became a source of major conflict. It was not easy to convey to the rest of the Labour movement how saving would really create – or safeguard – security, despite the references in the Crisis Programme to the exigencies of a new economic reality and the frequent analogies to the party's successful experiences of crisis management in the past. The cutbacks in the public sector signalled by the Crisis Group aroused protests in the Social Democratic party, protests that originated in the difficulty, at grass roots level, of distinguishing between the group's proposals and the policies of the Liberal government and the right-wing critique that social democracy had been taking issue with since the late 1970s.

Revolt had already threatened the movement in March 1981, when the Crisis Group circulated questions related to its programme for discussion at the regional level. The questions – would the party consider reductions in social benefits, longer working hours, rationalisation of the public sector? – gave rise to angry reactions about 'right-wing concessions'.[41] In February, an article was published in the social democratic daily *Arbetet*, in which the 'sextuplets', six economists led by Klas Eklund, urged drastic remedies for the Swedish economy and major savings in the public sector.[42] This article met with anger and prompted a reaction from the 'quintuplets', five expansion-oriented economists linked to the trade union movement, led by the trade union economist Carl Johan Åberg.[43] When the Crisis Group's questions arrived at the party's regional offices the following month, it was felt that the opinions of the sextuplets were being echoed by the party executive. At the 1981 social democratic conference, outraged speakers claimed that the crisis was being exaggerated and exploited.

> We should send these cuts back to where they came from, in other words, the theoretical world of liberal economists![44]

These protests were countered both by Ingvar Carlsson, the chairman of the Crisis Group, and Olof Palme, who stressed the programme's solid grounding in social democratic values and urged the party to rally behind it. Carlsson concluded the debate at the conference:

> Mr Chairman, I only want to add one more thing. Some speakers have given us a picture of Social Democracy that I do not quite recognise. They have talked about a U-turn, betrayal, the acceptance of the conditions of capitalism, and so on. The word 'retreat' has also been used . . . I have been trying to follow this debate. It is not clear to me what is meant ... We hope that after this congress we will have an economic programme that can lead us out of this economic crisis.[45]

For all the outraged responses to the questions and the debate at the congress, the Crisis Programme never did contain any specifics regarding exactly how or which cuts were to be made in the public sector under a social democratic government.[46]

In the 1982 election campaign, the Crisis Programme was presented as the Social Democrats' alternative to social dismantling. Immediately following their election victory, the party launched the third way policy with what later became known as the 16 per cent 'super-devaluation' of the Swedish krona.[47] During the following year the crisis policy was further pursued, with cuts in the public sector and restraint in wage negotiations. These gave rise to deep divisions between the Social Democratic party and the LO – the media quickly christened this conflict the War of the Roses and it is unclear if this war has ever quite come to an end. The LO opposed public sector cuts, demanded that the expansion policy to sustain employment and wage levels continue, and insisted that the party live up to the promises of continued social ambitions it had made in the electoral campaigns of the late 1970s.[48]

More reforms for our money!

In its 1981 Crisis Programme, the SAP had thus endorsed the critique of the SDE and taken its concept of cost efficiency and favoured problem-solving in cost-cutting on board. In doing so, it laid the foundations of a new social policy ideology. If the party's outlooks on social policy in the strong society were defined by the idea of a productive investment, here was a social policy ideology that was construed around the organising metaphor of cost.

Immediately after its return to power in 1982, the government began the work of reforming the public sector. A new ministry, the Ministry of Public Administration (*Civildepartmentet*), was established, and Bo Holmberg was appointed its head.[49] At the Ministry of Finance under Kjell-Olof Feldt, work commenced on increasing the cost efficiency of the production of social services.[50] The new government took over the ESO from the right-wing government, to act as an expert group on public policy within the Ministry of Finance.[51]

The ESO was now granted the status of a social democratic knowledge group, and its measurements of productivity and efficiency in social services became a central ingredient in social democratic policies for rationalisation and saving.[52] Its metaphors, its zeroing of productivity and its illustrations of the diminishing returns of social policy became the conceptual cornerstones of third way social policy ideology, just as the articulations of the SDE had provided a discursive platform for the Crisis Programme.

In 1985, the ESO provided the Ministry of Finance with a study of cost developments in social services and of productivity levels in childcare, home care, elderly care, and care of addicts and the physically challenged, that repeated the argument of the late 1970s and early 1980s. The study found that productivity in the social sector had declined by an average of 1.6 per cent per year between 1970 and 1980. While costs had risen to keep pace with the expansion of social services and growing social political ambitions during the 1970s, production in terms of the number of visits, clients, and children in nursery schools, for instance, had decreased. In other words, the development of productivity was unsatisfactory. The changes introduced during the 1970s that were discussed in Chapter 4, concerning, for example, the introduction of social planning to increase the structural impact of social policy (which was indeed embodied in the Social Welfare Act of 1982) in order to avoid social exclusion, create social efficiency and reduce social costs, were not considered to have any quantifiable impact on economic productivity and were therefore excluded from the study.[53] The ESO concluded that waning productivity suggested a decline in the returns on the capital invested in social policy.[54] Social services, like major aspects of production in other sections of the public sector, were therefore becoming more and more expensive. The logical conclusion of this assumption was that, if more resources were allocated, productivity would continue to decline until it would finally cease completely. This added greater weight to arguments for savings. At any rate, more resources would not have any significant impact on productivity.

In the same year, a special issue of the party review *Tiden* entitled 'Time to Start the Work of Reform Again!', dealt with reform of the public sector and the changes in social policy.[55] In it, the restructurings taking place were described as a process of renewal and long-term reform for the increased efficiency and productivity of public production. The long post-war phase of expansion and major investment was over. Now a 'rationalisation' phase was beginning, one that would bring about the more effective use of resources, and enable the party to maintain its social ambitions in a time of scarcity:

> Not more money for reforms but more reforms for our money![56]

The phrase 'more reforms for our money' clearly drew on the idea of decreasing marginal utility and it effectively conveyed the idea that the public sector had outlived its productive phase.

Renewing the people's home: a utopia of freedom of choice

Embarked on the third way, social democracy continued, as it had in the 1970s, to raise its sights where the 'weak' groups in society were concerned: the disabled, the elderly, the socially excluded. But these endeavours now took place within the framework of its crisis policy, which meant a continuous search for new ways of creating security that fitted in with the third way's emphasis on savings and budget restraint, while still providing individual welfare. While the Ministry of Finance sought to cut costs in the mid-1980s, after 1982 the party began the process of reformulating its social policy ideology around the watchword 'renewal' (*förnyelse*).

A manifesto for the 1984 conference, entitled *The future in the hands of the people* (*Framtiden i hela folkets händer*), was written by a group once again chaired by Ingvar Carlsson, who, in 1982, was given government responsibility for long-term decisions as Minister for the Future.[57] The group intended to write a programme for future policy, one that was based on the axioms of the crisis policy and the need for reconstruction of the Swedish economy, but was also bold enough to 'aim toward the future, beyond crisis policies'.[58] *The future in the hands of the people* dealt with the renewal of the public sector. 'Renewal' had to do with reforming the public sector in such a way that social ambitions could be maintained in times of crisis. The programme declared that third way social democracy faced a critical task, namely, the restoration of confidence in their party's ability to combine welfare policies with economic efficiency and the reconciliation of the goals of security and growth.[59] The implicit message of the programme was that this would require social democracy to abandon the ideological legacy behind the expansion of social policy and the public sector during the 1950s and 1960s. The programme was therefore devised as a form of settlement with the strong society's ideology of the 1950s and a break with its ideas about the relationship between growth and security.

This need to leave major parts of post-war ideology behind was apparent in the way in which Olof Palme presented the programme to the 1984 conference.

He described it as a new social democratic utopia,[60]

> a utopia that places people at the centre; not institutions, not laws, not structures, not paragraphs but only that – people. And that is probably where this programme has its greatest value. There is nothing really remarkable about this. It is a long-standing socialist tradition to speak of liberating the individual. In fact that is really what the fundamental tradition of socialism is, not that socialism should organise everything for people but that socialism should liberate people so that they themselves can fulfil their own lives, arrange their society in free and equal cooperation with other individuals. That is the basis of the fundamental social democratic concept of the citizen ... In this we also touch on the difference between our approach to people and a right-wing approach. We want to liberate individuals ... The *old authoritarian society* was based on institutions, bureaucracies, hierarchies, laws to provide a bulwark against what was believed to be an evil populace. We want these institutions to serve the people and to be governed by the people themselves. This is a slow and arduous development ... *The future in the hands of the people* is a conceptual programme that encourages renewal.[61]

This was a utopia that, to Palme, resembled neither the utopia of the right, in the form of the free market, nor the social democratic strong society, from which the party leadership seemed to want to distance themselves. The strong society was now described as a historical utopia, an outdated ideology of the past. A party pamphlet even spoke of building a new people's home, based on a social vision radically different from the one that had informed the construction of the welfare state in the period from the 1930s onwards.[62] Both Ingvar Carlsson and Olof Palme compared the Future Programme with the programmes that provided the ideological foundation for development of the public sector in the 1950s and early 1960s in *Policies for the future* (*Framtidens politik*, 1956) and *A society of choice* (*Valfrihetens samhälle*, 1962).[63]

The tasks that social democracy had historically entrusted to the public sector were now considered to have been completed. Whereas, in the 1950s, the former party leader Tage Erlander had understood security to mean the abolition of poverty and insecurity through extended societal responsibilities, security now referred to individual 'freedom of choice'.[64]

> Now, when a major expansion of the public sector has taken place, greater weight can be attached to another dimension of the social democratic concept of freedom. Now our efforts should be focused on allowing citizens greater choice in how to take advantage of the resources of the public sector.[65]

Freedom of choice was a concept that had an ideological basis in social democratic thinking. It was a central concept in Erlander's 1960s rhetoric.[66] But in the Future Programme, the concept was more clearly linked to neo-liberal language and the neo-liberal concept of freedom. Through a discussion that strongly echoed an Anglo-Saxon discourse historically alien to Swedish political thought, freedom of choice was described as transcending Erlander's 'negative' concept of freedom: freedom of choice was a 'positive' concept of freedom, one that dealt with the entitlement of individuals and their right to choose their own security and endow it with content.[67] Where Erlander's idea of freedom began in the collective, public responsibility of all for all, this was a notion of freedom that began in the individual responsibility for him/herself.

Ingvar Carlsson gave voice to this new concept of freedom of choice in his so-called Freedom speech in Göteborg in March 1983.[68] The Minister of Finance, Kjell Olof Feldt, also commented on freedom of choice in a polemic published in 1984. Erlander's theses on freedom from insecurity in a society of poverty had to be replaced by a positive concept of freedom in the developed welfare state – the freedom of the individual, not *from* social evil but *to* social good or, in Feldt's definition, the individual freedom to decide whether or not to 'have a drink'. This positive concept of freedom offered one way of avoiding excessive state intervention, whether it came in the guise of the selective and means-tested social policies that Feldt claimed would be the result of the neo-liberal alternative, or in the form of the paternalistic features and the abuse of official authority in the strong society. Feldt's polemic gave rise to a controversy in the party, because it was perceived as opening a door for the ideological possibility of new organisational forms, such as parent cooperatives and privatisation, but Feldt's discussion here was not so different from Palme's conference speech. When Palme spoke of the 'authoritarian society' to the 1985 congress, he alluded to the traditional social democratic punchbag, the old poor relief society, but he also clearly hinted that the authoritarian society was the strong society or the old people's home.[69] Feldt argued that freedom of choice must not result in an open market for services – this was where the social democratic utopia differed from that of the right. But security through freedom of choice would mean that people could freely choose what services to use and how these should be organised. Freedom of choice was about 'user influence' and 'client participation', democracy in social services and decentralisation of care.[70]

In other words, freedom of choice would offer another approach to enhancing social political ambitions, and in this way the concept of freedom of choice became the core of a new social policy ideology. Freedom of choice was a concept closely linked to efficiency and the 'husbanding' of resources.[71]

> [We must] always take into account the necessity of reducing budget deficits. In all circumstances therefore there must be a reallocation of resources and greater efficiency in the public sector ... One important task will be to attain this greater efficiency within the framework of existing resources and to provide better service in the public sector.[72]

In this way the concept of freedom of choice brought with it a new sense of balance and coherence between what was socially desirable and what the Crisis Programme claimed was economically necessary. Freedom of choice and cost efficiency became congruent, compatible objectives. In forging this link between efficiency and freedom of choice, a seemingly coherent frame of reference could be established; what was economically necessary within the confines of the crisis plan could also be represented as socially desirable, and freedom of choice as a means of ensuring individual security could also be articulated as a route to efficiency and growth. Nevertheless, the old relationship between security and growth still seemed intrinsically problematic.

The strategic role of the concept of freedom of choice in this process of renewal was demonstrated in the campaign, launched by the party executive after the 1985 election, entitled 'An offensive for social justice' (*Offensiv för rättvisa*). It was based on the ideas put forward in the Future Programme. Under the slogan 'A community in which we care about each other', different ways of providing care in decentralised services for the elderly, the physically challenged and the mentally ill were discussed. It was claimed that paucity of resources would have a 'vitalising' effect on the way these new solutions were designed. For example, far too many of the mentally ill were in care 'unnecessarily', when both the goals of allowing them freedom of choice and cutting costs could be achieved if they were able to stay in their own homes rather than remain in the institutions in which they were being treated. The changes that had been made in the Social Welfare Act in 1982, by which decentralised methods of social work, such as community outreach, had been introduced, were now referred to as sophisticated methods of meeting individual needs while also increasing efficiency.[73] The slogan 'A more equitable Sweden' provided an umbrella for a discussion by the party of ways to reduce dependency on social benefits. A publication entitled *Now we can move forward* boldly stated that freedom of choice was an instrument for achieving both efficiency and security.[74]

Social democracy had found a third way for social policy. This new social policy ideology subordinated 'security' to the concept of growth and the need to create economic efficiency by reducing social expenditure. Whereas the social policy offensive of the strong society was construed around the metaphor of investment, the third way's social policy ambitions were marked by its perception of social policy as a cost.

This pervasive cost metaphor brought about a shift of attitude in the social services groups and 'the weakest'. Freedom of choice, as a new and positive concept of freedom, also contained an element of individual responsibility. In the Future Programme's discussions of support for the physically challenged and measures to alleviate the increasing vulnerability that the crisis generated among immigrants in suburban areas, sole parents and the excluded, one of the conditions posed was that those affected had to participate if rehabilitation and social services were to be successful.[75] Freedom of choice, the programme asserted, did not mean that social democracy would accept exclusion, but it did involve the restitution of the personal responsibility of each individual for his or her own social situation.[76] This discussion contained unmistakeable traces of the incentives discourse put forward by the Swedish right.

To some extent, the discussion of responsibility involved a revival of the Strong society's approach to reinstating socially vulnerable groups in the production process. As in the ideology underlying strong society social policies, here too third way ideology emphasised participation in the labour market and the rehabilitation of groups in social services. But unlike the strong society's construction of these groups as potential production resources and productive investments, third way social policy ideology contained a construction of the groups in social policy as a cost, and moreover, a cost that could no longer be afforded. Defraying these costs required an active commitment by those in the care sector.

Our expensive welfare state

The social policy ideology of the third way, then, was based precisely on the articulation of social policy as a cost without productive effects, against which the trade union economists had protested in the debates of the SDE in the early 1980s. However, by the mid-1980s, the trade union economists also deferred to this outlook on social policy.

During the 1980s, a major enquiry on the welfare state got under way in the LO. This enquiry, chaired by Anna Hedborg, who worked with Meidner on the proposal for wage-earner funds in the 1970s and subsequently became the main architect of the 1994 pension reform, was initiated by the Municipal Workers' Union at its 1981 congress; in other words, in connection with the previously discussed report entitled *An overall view of efficiency*. In this report, two economists, Johansson and Kolk, defended a social approach to efficiency and productivity in the public sector and issued a warning against the 'zeroing of productivity' and productivity models taken from industry. The enquiry's final report was presented to the LO congress in 1986 under the title *The trade union movement and the welfare state*.[77]

This report was formulated as a defence of the Swedish welfare state and the principles underlying its famous universalism. It clearly felt that there was a need to remind people of the value basis of the Swedish welfare state and the socio-economic theory it historically drew upon. It patiently explained why the Swedish social policy model was better than the American 'poor relief' system. Swedish social policy was 'fair'. It protected the weak and created individual freedom. On the other hand, the report contained no discussion of the economic value of social services. In its attempts to counter the critique of the cost of the public sector, the report maintained that there was no evidence to prove that the Swedish model was economically inefficient.[78] However, it also did not quote any evidence to the contrary. Rather, the bulk of the report was devoted to a discussion of the problems of 'low productivity' in public production and the 'rising costs' of the public sector in the post-war period.

The report remained critical of mainstream measurements of productivity, but it was not overly assertive on this point.

> Knee-jerk assumptions that the rise in the productivity in the public sector is zero are, as a rule, erroneous, but they do tell us something important about the character of public services ... there is a tendency for expenditure to rise in large segments of the public sector ...[79]

In other words, they were, 'as a rule', wrong. But even though they were wrong, generally speaking, they could still 'tell us something important'. This important message was conveyed through the use of phrases and metaphors such as 'relative rise in costs', 'poor development of productivity', 'on the margin', 'the highest costs in the world' and 'more expensive', which effectively created an image of an increasingly burdensome public sector. Again, the template was the market, and the report adapted a managerial language that stood in stark contrast to previous LO reports.[80]

> It is a widely recognised truth from research in business administration that companies that are doing well and generating large profits tend to incur one or two unnecessary costs. This is often referred to as slack in their production ... During the period when the resources allocated to the public sector were rapidly rising all the time, it is more than likely that some slack developed in the system ... As the expansion of resources slowed down, productivity rose.[81]

Perhaps 'one or two follies' were committed during the post-war period, when resources were available. Perhaps austerity would compel a healthy process of rationalisation. Decentralisation and alternative operating procedures seemed to offer dividends both in terms of need gratification and productivity. The report cited several examples; for instance, the Board of Social Welfare had succeeded in reducing its staff; and the ongoing reform of psychiatric care and the return of the mentally ill to their homes and the community was providing greater security.[82] Strained resources had led to a revitalisation; 'one sets priorities and reflects and makes changes'.[83]

The view that the Swedish trade unions eventually adopted in *The trade union movement and the welfare state* corresponded perfectly to the approach to productivity and efficiency advocated by the SDE. Not surprisingly, it arrived at the conclusion previously advocated by the SDE in 1981, namely, that fewer resources would bring about more efficient social policies, in both social and economic terms. The consequence for the trade union movement was that they would have to stop demanding resources and rally instead behind discussions of renewal.[84]

The recurrent use of the concept of 'expensive' (*dyr*) illustrates the change in social democracy's understanding of social policy's economic role: to say that something is expensive is not only a reference to its cost; it is also an expression of the view that the cost is *unreasonable* in relation to the return. In other words, when something is expensive, it costs too much. As this description of reality gained a foothold also in the trade union movement, traditionally arch-modernisers but also defenders of the public sector, there were no longer any alternative articulations to this definition of social policy as a cost within Swedish social democracy.

Concluding remarks

The articulation of a third way in the early 1980s seemed to mark almost a complete turn around in Swedish social democracy's outlook on social policy. Once understood as a productive investment into growth, it was now spoken of in terms of a cost, that needed to be cut. Through the party's rereading of its main ideologue Wigforss, saving became an instrument for social reform, the fundamental means of safeguarding security in a time of economic trouble. To this extent the third way was a culmination of the gradual slippages in the grass roots of party rhetoric since the late 1960s. Alva Myrdal's words from 1969, 'we can afford a generous attitude to those who do not succeed in our society' acquired another layer of meaning as the Crisis Programme stated that not only were there groups in society who were less productive than others, but moreover that these could in fact no longer be afforded. In third way ideology, growth decisively displaced security as the dominant element of party discourse, as the overarching ideological goal of the third way was the re-creation of economic efficiency. In this new ideology, security lost its strategic role for growth, and the party's social theory became a question of the adaptation of social objectives to growth. Freedom of choice, as a new element for individual security and emancipation, was a concept whose meaning came from the economic. Freedom of choice was a concept devised to fit the party's new doctrines of cost efficiency and marginal utility. Freedom of choice, despite its strong links to Erlander's post-war discourse, contained fundamentally different notions of the relationship between individual and collective responsibility than did the ideology of the strong society. Public responsibility for individual security was represented as having reached maturity. The time was ripe to give some responsibility back to people. This notion opened the door to a debate, in the years to come, on the role of both market and civil society in the Swedish welfare state. The renewed people's home, to that extent, was a utopia very different from the original people's home, which did not recognise either the market or the civil society as separate entities from society, but incorporated them into one vast notion of the social good in the concept of *samhälle.*

Notes

1 Mullard, M. and Spicker, P., 1998, *Social policy in a changing society*, Routledge, New York.
2 Hall 1993; Hall, P., 1986, *Governing the economy. The politics of state intervention in Britain and France*, Oxford University Press, New York; Hall, S. and Jacques, M. (eds), 1983, *The politics of Thatcherism*, Lawrence and Wishart, London; Katz 1989; Mishra, 1984.
3 For instance, a lecture by Friedman was published by Timbro in 1977; see Friedman, M., 1977, *Välfärdsstatens myter: föredrag inför företagsekonomiska och nationalekonomiska föreningen i Skåne den 20 juni 1977*, Timbro, Stockholm, and Hayek, F., 1983, *Frihetens grundvalar*, Ratio, Stockholm.
4 Palme was a controversial character in the Swedish political landscape, depicted from early on in his political career as a class traitor (he came from the Swedish upper class) and arrogant *besserwisser* by right-wing observers. In the 1980s the 'hate campaigns' against Palme intensified. See Björk, G., ongoing research, Institute for Contemporary History, Stockholm.
5 Palme 1987 pp. 45–62, '*Militärdiktaturen och marknaden i skön förening*'.

6 Hugemark, A., 1994, *Den fängslande marknaden. Ekonomerna och den offentliga sektorn*, Arkiv, Lund.
7 Bergström, H., 1987, *Rivstart? Om övergången från opposition till regering*, Tiden, Stockholm, p. 83.
8 Ingvar Carlsson in a speech in Sundsvall, October 11 1980; Ingvar Carlsson archives, vol. 2.11.4.
9 Ingvar Carlsson in a speech in Norrköping, June 8, 1980, Blekinge, March 21, 1981, Ingvar Carlsson archives vol. 2.11.4. Ingvar Carlsson in a debate with Ulf Adelsohn, May 1 1981, Ingvar Carlsson archives vol. 2.11.5. See Olof Palme's speech in the Olof Palme archives vol. 4.2.160, and Private Member's Bill 1980/81:1136 p. 31.
10 Government Bill 1979/1980:1 and SAP bill 1979/1980:69; SAP bill 1979/1980:1067, 1980/81:71; election manifesto August 9 1979 and the so-called 100–Days Programme, August 30 1979, in the Olof Palme archives series 4.2 vol. 147. Poster reproduced in *LO-tidningen*, 17, 1982, p. 15.
11 Ryner 2001; Stråth 1998; Pontusson 1992; Benner 1997.
12 It has been suggested that Erik Åsbrink and Klas Eklund were the motivating forces of this group. See Bergström 1987 and Lindvall 2004.
13 Memorandum May 14 1981, SDE archives, vol. F 11 A 020.
14 Ibid.
15 'Neo-liberalism in practice' was published by the SDE in April 1982.
16 Memorandum, November 10 1980, SDE archives vol. F 11 A 019.
17 Gösta Rehn, November 22 1980, at a seminar on the public sector, 'Solidarity in small and large collectives' (*Solidariteten i de små och stora kollektiven*, p. 12, SDE archives F 11 A Vol. 019. Cf. the observation made by Bo Holmberg, November 22 1980.
18 Memorandum, June 18 1980 (Arne Granholm); Memorandum June 8, 1980, headed 'Does Sweden Pay?' (*Lönar sig Sverige?*); Memorandum, May 20 1980, SDE archives vol. F 11 A 019.
19 Memorandum, June 8 1980, SDE archives vol. F 11 A 019.
20 This division is often depicted as a division between academic and trade union economists, or between austerity and expansion economists.
21 Memorandum, June 18 1980 and the duplicated publication by the SDE in 1981 of 'Solidarity in Small and Large Collectives'. In April 1985 a new seminar was arranged on the public sector. SDE archives, vol. F 11 A 020.
22 Transcript, November 22 1980, SDE archives vol. F 11 A 019.
23 Memorandum, November 22 1980, SDE archives vol. F 11 A 019. See Eklund, K., 1981, 'Är Keynes verkligen död? Introduktion till den nya nationalekonomin', *Tiden*, 7, pp. 503–513; Eklund, K., 1982, *Den bistra sanningen. Om Sveriges ekonomi och de kommande bistra åren*, Tiden, Stockholm. Cf. Kjell-Olof Feldt in *Tiden* 1980, 'Inför 1980–talet: arbete, sparsamhet och hushållning', p. 228, and Åberg, C.-J., 1981, *Keynes på 1980–talet, kan sysselsättningen räddas?*, Tiden, Stockholm.
24 Bo Holmberg and Sten Johansson, November 22 1980, SDE archives, vol. F 11 A 019.
25 Swedish Municipal Workers' Union (1980). Undated draft memorandum, June 8 1980, SDE archives, vol. F 11 A 019.
26 Council of Nordic Trade Unions 1980 pp. 9, 17.
27 Meidner, R., 1982, 'Den offentliga sektorns expansion', *Hotad sektor* p. 21. Swedish Municipal Workers' Union, 1980, *En helhetssyn på effektiviteten.*
28 Ds B 1980:17; Ds B 1982:3.
29 Hugemark 1994.

30 See for instance Ds Fi 1985:3.
31 The members of the Crisis Group were Ingvar Carlsson, Kjell-Olof Feldt, Rune Molin, Leni Björklund, Erik Åsbrink, Odd Engström, Ann-Marie Lindgren and Per-Olov Edin.
32 SAP 1981a, *Framtid för Sverige, förslag*, p. 39.
33 SAP 1981a, p. 32f. Cf. Olof Palme material in the Olof Palme archive, vol. 4.2.170.
34 See for instance Olof Palme's speech at the conference of the Metalworkers' Union in June 1981, Palme 1987 p. 51.
35 SAP 1981a, p. 30.
36 SAP 1981a, p. 24. Cf. Wigforss, 1932, p. 7
37 SAP 1981a, p. 24. Cf. Olof Palme's speech to the Riksdag in the debate on public policy, February 3 1982, the Olof Palme archive, vol. 4. 2.163.
38 Wigforss 1932.
39 SAP 1981a, p. 52.
40 SAP 1981a, s. 30.
41 Letter from Sten Andersson to the district parties, March 12 1981, with the material from the Crisis Group and the responses received, SAP Crisis group archive, vol. F 11 A 049.
42 *Arbetet*, February 18 1981, SAP collection of press cuttings, Series Ö 1 A vol. 249.
43 *Arbetet*, February 24 1981, SAP collection of press cuttings, Series Ö 1 A vol. 253.
44 SAP 1981 conference protocol pp. B 8, 17–25.
45 SAP 1981 conference protocol p. B 170.
46 SAP 1981b, *Framtid för Sverige, handlingslinjer för att föra Sverige ur krisen*, Feldt; K.-O., 1991, *Alla dessa dagar*, Norstedts, Stockholm, p. 26.
47 Jonung, L., 2000, *Looking ahead through the rearview mirror, Swedish stabilisation policies as a learning process 1970–1995, a summary*, ESO, Stockholm (English summary of Jonung 1999, *Med backspegeln som kompass*, Ds 1999:9, Stockholm); Ryner 2002; Benner 1997.
48 Johansson, A. and Magnusson, L., 1998, *LO, Andra halvseklet*, Atlas, Stockholm, p. 316.
49 Mellbourn 1986. See Holmberg, B., 1986, *Nu våras det!*, Civildepartementet, Stockholm.
50 Mellbourn 1986 p. 19; Feldt 1991 p. 41.
51 Mellbourn 1986 p. 29.
52 ESO annual reports (*verksamhetsberättelser*) 1981/1982, 1982/1983, 1983/1984. See Ds Fi 1984:2; Ds Fi 1984:8; Ds Fi 1984:19; Ds Fi 1985:11; Ds Fi 1986:13; Ds Fi 1986:16; Ds Fi 1987:2.
53 Ds Fi 1985:4 pp. 2f., 5f., 47
54 Ds Fi 1985:4.
55 *Tiden* 5–6 1985 p. 262.
56 *Tiden* 5–6 1985 p. 262.
57 This group also included Rolf Alsing, Åke Edin, Eva Gillström, Gunnel Hedman, Sven Hulterström, Bert Lundin, Sigvard Marjasin, Rune Molin, Yrsa Stenius, and Margot Wallström. Its secretariat included Kjell Larsson, Anna Hedborg and Lars Hjalmarsson.
58 SAP 1984 conference protocol p. A 102.
59 SAP 1984a, *Framtiden i hela folkets händer*, p. 28.
60 SAP 1984 conference protocol pp. A 108–109, D 261–263.
61 SAP 1984 conference protocol pp. D 262–263.

62 For the original idea of the people's home in the form of the universal welfare state see Chapter 1.
63 SAP, Renewing the people's home (*Förnyelse av folkhemmet*).
64 SAP 1984a. Cf. Erlander 1954, 1956, 1962; Lewin 1967; Ruin 1986; Tilton 1990.
65 SAP 1984a, p. 69.
66 See Erlander 1962.
67 The distinction between the concepts of positive and negative freedom can be traced from the philosopher Isaiah Berlin; see Berlin, I., 1969, 'Two concepts of liberty', in Goodin, R. and Pettit, P. (eds), 1997, *Contemporary political philosophy, an anthology*, Blackwell, Oxford.
68 Carlsson 1983, 'Freedom and faith in the future' (*Frihet och framtidstro*) speech. See also Carlsson, I. and Anell, L., 1985, *Individens frihet och framtid i välfärdssamhället*, LO, Stockholm, and Färm, G., 1991, *Carlsson – en samtalsbok med Ingvar Carlsson*, Tiden, Stockholm.
69 Feldt, K.-O., 1984, *Samtal med Feldt, Berndt Ahlqvist och Lars Engqvist intervjuar finansministern*, Tiden, Stockholm, pp. 21, 25, 99–104. See Feldt 1991 p. 183f.
70 SAP 1984 conference protocol p. D 261.
71 SAP 1984a p. 28.
72 SAP 1984a p. 39.
73 SAP 1983, *Kommunal socialpolitik.*
74 Material for the 'offensive for justice' campaign ('A more equitable Sweden', 'A joint sector for security and service'), SAP collection of publications; SAP 1984b, *Slå vakt om solidariteten.* Cf. Holmberg 1986.
75 SAP 1984a p. 42.
76 SAP 1984a pp. 14, 52.
77 LO 1986, *Fackföreningsrörelsen och den offentliga sektorn.* The material on which the enquiry was based was published in the series *Offentliga samtal* (*Public conversations*) during 1985 and 1986.
78 The basis for this could be found in Korpi, W., 1985, *Marknad eller politik? Om de politiska alternativen i 1980–talets Sverige*, LO, Stockholm.
79 LO 1986 p. 17.
80 LO 1986 p. 149.
81 LO 1986 p. 149.
82 LO 1986 p. 149. The opening up of the mental institutions has become one of the most contested reforms in Sweden.
83 LO 1986 p. 147.
84 Ibid.

7
Concluding remarks

This book has addressed a central aspect of Swedish reformism, the idea that economic growth and individual security are two fundamentally connected economic and social processes that need to be kept together. On the one hand, Swedish social democracy has stressed capitalism as a system producing a social good, compatible with individual welfare, but on the other, it has given an explicit role to the welfare state in that process. To an extent, this duality between economic dynamism, on the one hand, and individual security and welfare, on the other, is a general dilemma to social democracy in its various national contexts because of its historical acceptance of capitalism. Interpretations of exactly how this relationship between economic efficiency and individual security should be understood, however, differ between social democracies in different national contexts and different historical settings. This book has dealt specifically with what I have argued is a particularly Swedish idea, central to what Esping-Andersen once described as the social-democratic welfare regime and a characteristic of the ideology of the SAP, namely the idea that not only can growth be steered towards individual security, but that security and the welfare state also has a central role for an efficient economy and the creation of growth. Security, in this interpretation, was not a cost for mollifying the disruptive social effects of industrial capitalism, but an investment into more productive forms of social organisation. This notion of security as the foundation of successful economic change can be said to be the very meaning of the term security in SAP rhetoric. For instance, the Swedish interpretation of flexibility, in the contemporary process of labour market restructuring, is 'security in change' (*trygghet i förändring*), and sets security as the condition for labour mobility and individual adaptation.[1]

I have argued that this interplay between economic and social objectives in social democratic language takes the form of a duality, by which the meaning of the term *trygghet* is not only social, but spills over into the economic sphere, by which the concept also derives meaning from the economic and is inherently understood in relation to interpretations of the needs of production. The famous Swedish universalism drew on a productivism that on the one hand strengthened social citizenship and led to the institutionalisation of social policy as an integral part of the Swedish model, but on the other hand also provided a latent conditionality to social citizenship and a constant differentiation between groups in and outside of the labour market.

This socio-economic theory was drawn up in the 1930s crisis and the following replacement of ideas of nationalisation of production with functional socialism, targeted consumption and welfare reform as the way to socialism. It remained a core idea in SAP ideology in the post-war period, giving rise to an economic language around welfare reform, social policy and the public sector, which was construed around the central notion of investment. To this extent, the idea of the productive role of the individual was an integral part of the post-war Swedish middle way model, giving rise to a much broader conceptualisation of the role of social justice than in liberal discourses. Social justice was not, essentially, a question of redistribution of resources created elsewhere in the economy, but a question of creating resources. This can be described as a theory of value, and a notion of progress, that drew on the idea that economic and social advances were dependent on one another, and that they had to be carefully balanced. As we have seen, the very idea of redistribution as a transfer of resources from productive to less productive sectors or groups in society was a step away from this conception of the productive role of social spending.

I have argued in the previous pages that this notion of an umbilical link between security and growth is a core in Swedish reformism, to the extent that it is possible to speak of a crisis of social democracy in the periods when this relationship has been questioned and put under pressure from alternative articulations from both left and right. The central narrative of this book has been a historical account of two such periods of critique and crisis, when this relationship is questioned and reforged. The late 1960s was a crisis for the social democratic concept of growth, following a clash between social democratic ideology and new interpretations of social reality, and the early 1980s was a period of crisis for the SAP's idea of security, following a similar clash between ideology and new images of the economic world. These periods of struggle and rearticulation have been seen as leading up to the changes in discourse of the 1980s. Indeed the attempts to lay out a third way in the Crisis Programme and the later developments in the 1980s seemed to mark almost a turnaround in the SAP's historical outlook on the productive role of welfare. The Labour movement, from the mid-1980s, and also the LO, accepted the idea that the public sector was consumption and not production and that there was a tangible distinction between these two spheres. A historic language of social efficiency, productive consumption, and social investment was silenced in favour of a new economic language organised around the notion of cost, cost efficiency, and the decreasing marginal utility of the welfare state.

What I have argued however, is that this did not take place as a break with a classical ideological heritage, following the rise of neo-liberalism in the late 1970s and early 1980s, but that modernisation is a question of gradual transfers of meaning where interpretations of new experiences of the surrounding world are added to existing layers. It is not possible to see the transformation of social democracy as a transition from a stable post-war ideology, organised around classical social democratic values of equality, solidarity and security, to a market driven third way ideology. The origins of the Swedish third way must be set both in a longer historical perspective and in a broader spectre of the carriers of discourse and political change. Specifically, I have pointed to continuities from the new left of the 1960s to the new right of the 1980s and to the way that in the Swedish context these developments took place within social democracy. As has been shown in the previous pages, there is a more or less constant process of renegotiation of the fundamental meaning of security (and growth) throughout the post-war period, a renegotiation that departs in the fundamental tension between these two aspects of development. Even in the relatively stable ideology of the strong society, there was a certain awareness of negative social effects of the expansion of production, and it was this tension that led to struggle and rearticulation in the period following. In a sense, it is fair to say that the relative hegemony of the SAP in the post-war period coexisted with increasing antagonism around the welfare state throughout this same period, an antagonism first concerned with problems of maturity and affluence, and then with a return to scarcity and austerity. Neither the meaning of growth nor of security is hegemonic during these decades – but in constant rearticulation. The same is of course true of other central ideological concepts such as equality or solidarity.

Specifically, my interest has been in the relationship between the notions of growth and security, as means and ends to each other in a hierarchy between the economic and the social in social democratic ideology. Ultimately, this book has argued that the third way claim that the process of ideological modernisation is a 'mere' question of pragmatically recalibrating means to the same ends is misconceived and banalises the way that this process of revisionism often goes well beyond questions of technical means to questions of the hierarchy between overarching ideological objectives. It has argued that the essence of ideological change, rather, is exactly in that rearticulation of means to ends and in the hierarchy between central ideological concerns. This has been the focal point of this study.

It is possible to discern, from this perspective, three very different ideologies in Swedish social democracy during this period, all of which have been discussed in the previous pages. The strong society drew on the idea that growth and security were coherent ends and gave the expanding welfare state a central place in its growth strategy. The 1970s, in contrast, were preoccupied with the idea of social exclusion and rising inequalities as a negative effect of industrial growth, and shifted the hierarchy between security and growth to the point that individual security was sometimes allowed to take precedence over the central place of growth in social democratic ideology. The 1980s construction of a hesitant third way ideology reversed this development and reasserted the ideological standing of growth. The third way's ideas of the creation of growth, however, were radically different from the ideas of growth of the strong society, as it rejected the idea that security created growth. These changes were all understood by social democracy as a matter of adaptation to external circumstances and they were all dressed in a pragmatic language around the limitations of social reform in a changing economic and social world. Yet they seem to embody three different worldviews, and three different philosophies of the interplay between economy and society, and of the relationship between individual needs and social democratic politics. The emphasis on public responsibility and collective solidarity as the precondition for individual emancipation and economic dynamism in the 1950s was replaced, in the 1970s, with a radicalisation that focused on the standing of individual social rights and, to some extent, turned against the collectivism of the labour movement. This 1970s discourse provided an important part of the underpinnings of third way policies as they developed in the early 1980s. Perhaps the most important change in this respect is the replacement of the optimistic but possibly naive faith in progress as a step-by-step process towards the completion of the people's home of the 1950s, with a hesitant and even fearful outlook on change as deeply unpredictable.

The Swedish third way was a hesitant experimentation with a new social democratic language around economic and social affairs based on choice, cost efficiency, and individual responsibility. It never went as far as, for instance, its British equivalent. As the international centre-left project came about in the mid-1990s, Swedish social democracy had already fallen out of love with the idea of the third way, despite Göran Persson's backing of the Blair-Schröder document.[2] Today, Swedish social democracy is again stressing its idea of a strong relationship between growth and security as a mark of distinction between the Swedish *folkhem*-model and other models in the debate on the future of the European social model, and against US-style workfare capitalism. Others are looking to this Swedish idea, too. The Lisbon strategy, which Swedish social democracy put a lot of hope to and has sometimes claimed as the social democratisation of Europe, defines social policy as a 'productive factor' and sets out a vision of the interplay between economic dynamism and social cohesion.[3] New Labour's claim that what's fair is also efficient, and its discourse of social investment, is also reminiscent of a Swedish idea of social policy as a productive investment.[4] However, both the European discourse and the British discourse have so far differed fundamentally from the historical Swedish discourse around social policy. Both on the European level and in British politics, the productive aspect of social policy has been defined by what is termed 'make work pay' and an incentives approach to 'dependency' that stands in rather sharp contrast to a Swedish reluctance to talk about incentives and a stress, rather, in Swedish discourse on the close interplay between benefits and productive participation over the life cycle. Moreover, the stress, both in European and British discourse, has clearly been on the responsibility side of the social contract. It is by strengthening individual obligation that social policy will be made a productive factor. The discourse around means such as welfare to work and the new deal has been fundamentally different in this respect from the historical discourse around Swedish active labour market policies in their emphasis on individual responsibility and a language of competition that is far from the language of solidarity and the ideas of public and corporate responsibility that surrounded the Rehn-Meidner model. In Sweden, productivism was conceptualised, historically, as a right to participate productively, and it is rights that are defined as productive. Maybe this is splitting hairs of discourse, but it certainly suggests very different ideas of the social contract and very different outlooks both on the role of politics and on the motivations of individuals. In essence, Swedish discourse says that security is the precondition of change, for providing individual security in times of disruptive change; whereas New Labour discourse argues that individuals have to be induced and coerced to accept the process of change as the precondition of security. This is in fact the central meaning of modernisation in Anglo-Saxon third way discourse. To this extent, the social investment discourse of New Labour from the mid-1990s onwards draws on an almost diametrically different value content than did the SAP's historical discourse around the welfare state. Recently, there has been a new-found British interest in Sweden that has been more concerned with ideas of security and public responsibility as a precondition for successful economic change.[5] Gordon Brown recently spoke on the role of security for change, which seems to stand in some contrast to how he has previously emphasised that there can be no security without change, and spoke with the Swedish Minister of Finance Pär Nuder of common outlooks on the European social model at the SAP's annual economic seminar in Almedalen in the summer of 2005.[6] Where this will lead remains to be seen.

Also Swedish social democratic discourse seems to be in a stage of transition. Today, Swedish social democratic politicians stress continuity with the ideological heritage from Wigforss and Erlander, but they would be more reluctant to speak of the Crisis Programme in 1981, and they might even say that the changes of discourse introduced in the 1980s were not ideologically important.[7] The process of financial restructuring that took place after 1992 is similarly understood as a process of pragmatic crisis-solving that did not change the values of the model in the bigger picture, but rather, saved it for the future.[8] Certainly Sweden has emerged on the other side of the 1990s as a fairly solid welfare state. But has social democratic ideology? The question is, what does it mean when the party leadership today speaks of 'productive welfare', after the individualisation of the 1960s, the new public management of the 1980s and the politics of retrenchment of the 1990s? What, indeed, is the meaning of *trygghet*, with falling levels of employment, growing social exclusion, and a growing social divide between ethnic Swedes and 'new Swedes'? In my view, the party's contemporary discourse of productive welfare cannot be seen as a straightforward and unproblematic return to an ideological heritage. Persson, in his address of a policy network meeting in Budapest in 2004, does not mean the same thing as Erlander did in debates with the Liberal party on the public sector in the late 1950s, and indeed Erlander did not mean the same thing in the 1950s as Myrdal did in the debate with the old Stockholm School in the Depression. The concepts may be the same or similar; the content is not necessarily so. The crucial issue for the

SAP in the campaign before the parliamentary elections in September 2006 is the lack of an articulated social democratic future vision that is capable of fending off a rising Swedish centre-right alliance between the Conservative party, the Centre party and the Liberal party. In its rhetoric, the party insists that welfare allowances and unemployment benefits are productive, but speaks more quietly of the growing problem of unemployment, the political responsibility for meaningful activation, and the individual right to work, partly because of its unwillingness to take an incentives approach to problems of long-term sick leaves and incapacity. To this extent, it seems to me that productive universalism, as a post-war ontology and ideology – that is as a worldview of how economy and society are related but also a normative belief in how economy and society should be linked by political intervention – has been replaced by a strategic discursive defence of the welfare state and social democratic ideology, on the one hand, but a failure to truly address the productive potential of all, on the other. This is, in a sense, a return to a historical legacy, but it also draws on the legacy of the third way experiment in the 1980s and the party seems to be uncomfortably stuck in the gap between these two legacies.

To conclude, I would suggest that a central point of change in Swedish social democratic thought, discussed in the previous pages, is the gradual acceptance in party ideology of a group in Swedish society that is not productive and that constantly falls behind. The empirical observation of the existence of such a group, as happened in the 1960s, and the rhetorical construction of it in a political discourse drawing on descriptions such as 'weak', 'handicapped', and 'those who can't cope', are of course two interrelated things. The emergence of this group – and the gradual acceptance of its existence in social democratic discourse – is a major challenge to the logic of productive universalism that was discussed in Chapter 1. A group that cannot be presumed to participate on the same terms as others is a burden on the solidarity of others, and the question then is how to create space within notions of solidarity for such differences. As was also set out in Chapter 1, a difference between Swedish social democracy and Anglo-Saxon discourse is that Swedish social democracy has always been very cautious to speak in terms of a dichotomy between rights and responsibilities or of deserving and undeserving poor. Rather it has stressed the productive potential of all and the right of all to participate on terms adapted to individual circumstance, and circumstances defined by the course of the life cycle. I believe this is a perfectly viable and desirable strategy also for the future of the Swedish welfare state, but it hinges, in my view, on the creation of a discourse and policy that does address the productive potential of all, and does not fall into the trap of a predetermined outlook on 'the weak', those that party rhetoric today talks of in terms of the non profitable (*icke lönsamma*), those left behind in the transformation from an industrial economy to an economy based on knowledge and information.[9]

Notes

1 See Murhem, S., forthcoming.
2 Blair, T. and Schröder, G., 2000, 'Europe: the third way – die neue mitte', in Hombach, B. (ed.), *The third way – die neue mitte*, pp. 160–172.
3 *The Lisbon European council – an agenda of economic and social renewal for Europe*, Göran Persson to the policy network meeting in Budapest 2004, www.policy-network.net.
4 Brown, G., 1994, *Fair is efficient*, Fabian Society, London.
5 Taylor, R., 2005, *Sweden's new social democratic model. Proof that a better world is possible*, Compass, London.
6 Brown speech to the Labour Party conference 2004, and Brown speech in Almedalen 2005, see www.sap.se.
7 This has been suggested to me by several leading social democrats.
8 See the Prime Minister Göran Persson's account of the 1990s: Persson, G., 1997, *Den som är satt i skuld är icke fri*, Atlas, Stockholm.
9 Socialdemokraterna, *Partiprogram 2001*.

Bibliography

Åberg, C.-J., 1981, *Keynes på 80–talet: kan sysselsättningen räddas?*, Tiden, Stockholm.

Adler-Karlsson, G. 1967, Funktionssocialism. Ett alternativ till kommunism och kapitalism, Verdandi debatt, Prisma, Stockholm.

Åkerman, N., 1974, 'Kommunismen och kapitalismen har kört fast, då är den demokratiska socialismen ett alternativ', *Aftonbladet* 1974–10–04 pp. 10–11.

Arndt, H.W., 1987, *Economic development. The history of an idea*, University of Chicago Press, Chicago.

Andersson, J., 2005, 'A productive social citizenship? The metaphor of productive social policies in the European tradition' in Stråth, B. and Magnusson, L., eds, *A European social citizenship? Future preconditions in historical light*, PIE, Peter Lang, Brussels.

Andersson J., 2005, 'The People's library and the electronic workshop', paper to the second conference *Rethinking social democracy*, Swansea, April 2005.

Andersson, J., 2006, 'Choosing futures: The construction of Swedish futures studies 1967–1972', *International review of social history*, 51 pp. 277–295.

Anshelm, J., 1995, *Socialdemokratin och miljöfrågan*, Symposion, Stockholm.

Aspling, S., 1970, *Socialpolitiskt reformarbete för ökad jämlikhet*, Socialdemokraterna, Stockholm.

Aspling, S., 1971, *Socialpolitiken – trygghetspolitiken*, Socialdemokraterna, Stockholm.

Aspling, S., 1999, *Med Erlander och Palme*, Tiden, Stockholm.

Ayres, R., 1998, *Turning point. The end of the growth paradigm*, Earthscan, London.

Beilharz, P. and Nyland, C., 1998, *The Webbs, fabianism and feminism: fabianism and the political economy of everyday life*, Aldershot, Ashgate.

Berlin, I., 1969, 'Two Concepts of Liberty', in Goodin, R. and Pettit, P., eds, 1997, *Contemporary political philosophy. An anthology*, Blackwell, Oxford.

Berman, S., 1998, *The social democratic moment*, Harvard University Press, Boston.

Benner, M., 1997, *The politics of growth. Economic regulation in Sweden 1930–1994*, Arkiv, Lund.

Bergqvist, C. and Nyberg, A., 2002, 'Welfare state reconstruction and childcare in Sweden', in Michel, S., ed., *Childcare at the crossroads*, Routledge, New York.

Bergström, H., 1987, *Rivstart? Om övergången från opposition till regering*, Tiden, Stockholm.

Björkman, J., 2001, *Vård för samhällets bästa*, Carlssons, Stockholm.

Blair, T., 1998, *The third way – new politics for the new century*, Fabian Society, London.

Blair, T. and Schröder, G., 2000, 'Europe: the third way – die neue mitte', in Hombach,

B., ed., *The third way – die neue mitte*, Polity Press.

Blyth, M., 2002, *Great transformations. Economic ideas and institutional change in the 20th century*, Harvard University Press, Boston.

Blomqvist, P. 2004, *Ideas and policy convergence. Health care reform in the Netherlands and Sweden in the 1990s*, doctoral dissertation, Columbia University, New York.

Blomqvist, P. and Rothstein, B., 2000, *Välfärdsstatens nya ansikte*, Agora, Stockholm.

Bok, S., 1991, *Alva Myrdal. A daughter's memoir*, Addison-Wesley, Reading, MA.

Boréus, K., 1994, *Högervåg. Nyliberalism och kampen om språket i svensk offentlig debatt 1969–1989*, Borea, Stockholm.

Borkowski, T., ed., 1991, *Social Policies in a time of transformation*, Goethe Institut and Jagiellonian University, Krakow.

Brandt, W., Kreisky, B. and Palme, O., 1975, *Briefe und gespräche 1972 bis 1975. Demokratischer sozialismus in theorie und praxis*, Europeische Verlagsanstalt, Frankfurt.

Broberg, G. and Tydén, M., 1996, 'Eugenics in Sweden, efficient care', in Broberg, G., and Roll-Hansen, N., eds, *Eugenics in the welfare state*, Michigan State University Press, Michigan.

Brown, G., 1994, *Fair is efficient*, Fabian Society, London.

Byrne, D., 1999, *Social exclusion*, Open University Press, London.

Callaghan, J., 2000, *The retreat of social democracy*, Manchester University Press, Manchester.

Carlson, A., 1990, *The Swedish experiment in family politics. The Myrdals and the interwar population crisis*, Transaction, New Brunswick.

Carlsson, B., 1991, 'The Long Retreat: Gustav Cassel and Eli Heckscher on the New Economics of the 1930s', in Jonung, L., ed., *The Stockholm school of economics revisited*, Cambridge University Press, Cambridge.

Carlsson, B. 1994, *The state as a monster. Gustav Cassel and Eli Heckscher on the role of the state*, University Press of America, Boston.

Carlsson, B. and Wadensjö, E., 1991, 'The Committee on unemployment and the Stockholm school', in Jonung, L., ed., *The Stockholm School of economics revisited*, Cambridge University Press, Cambridge.

Carlsson, I. and Anell, L., 1985, *Individens frihet och framtid i välfärdssamhället*, LO/Offentliga Samtal, Stockholm.

Carlsson, I., 2003, *Så tänkte jag. Politik och dramatik*, Hjalmarson och Högeberg, Stockholm.

Cassel, G., 1902, *Socialpolitiken*, Gebers, Stockholm.

Clemence, W. and Mahon, R., eds., 1994, *Swedish social democracy. A model in transition*, Studies in Political Economy, Toronto.

Club of Rome, 1976, *The limits to growth*, Paris.

'Dags att dra igång reformarbetet igen', *Tiden* 3:1985.

Ds [Departementsserien] S 1969:11, *Lagstiftning om sociala nämnder i kommunerna*

Ds U 1971:4, *Mål och riktlinjer för verksamheten vid ett institut för social forskning: förslag avgivet av organisationskommittén för ett institut för social forskning.*

Ds In 1971:16, *Kompendium om låginkomstutredningen.*

Ds In 1972:19, *Arbetsgruppen för låginkomstfrågor, Rapport.*

Ds S 1973:1, *Resurser och organisation för forskning och utvecklingsarbete inom socialsektorn, Delrapport 1.*

Ds S 1973:8, *Resurser och organisation för forskning och utvecklingsarbete inom socialsektorn, Delrapport 2.*

Ds Ju 1979:1, *Vägar till ökad välfärd. Betänkande av särskilda näringspolitiska delegationen.*
Ds Ju 1979:2, *Vägar till ökad välfärd, Expertbilaga.*
Ds B 1980:17, *Bättre beslutsunderlag för budgetpolitiken. Rapport från utredningen om forsknings- och utvecklingsinsatser rörande offentlig ekonomi,* Budgetdepartementet/ESO.
Ds B 1982:3, ESO, *Perspektiv på besparingspolitiken.*
Ds Fi 1984:2, ESO, *Vem utnyttjar den offentliga sektorns tjänster?*
Ds Fi 1984:8, ESO, *Är subventioner effektiva?*
Ds Fi 1984:19, ESO, *Återkommande kostnads och prestationsjämförelser – en metod att främja effektivitet i offentlig tjänsteproduktion.*
Ds Fi 1985:4, ESO, *Produktions-, kostnads- och produktivitetsutveckling inom den sociala sektorn 1970–1980.*
Ds Fi 1985:11, ESO, *Sociala avgifter – problem och möjligheter inom färdtjänst och hemtjänst.*
Ds Fi 1986:13, ESO, *Offentliga tjänster – sökarljus mot produktivitet och användare.*
Ds Fi 1986:16, ESO, *Socialbidrag. Bidragsmottagarna: antal och inkomster, Socialbidragen i bidragssystemet.*
Ds Fi 1987:2, ESO, *Att leva på avgifter – vad innebär en övergång till avgiftsfinansiering?*
Denvall, V. and Salonen, T., 1997, *Välfärdens operatörer. Om social planering i brytningstid,* Boréa, Umeå.
Driver, S. and Martell, L., 1998, *New Labour: politics after Thatcherism,* Polity Press, Cambridge.
Elander, I., 1978, *Det nödvändiga och det önskvärda,* Arkiv, Lund.
Elmbrant, B., 1989, *Palme,* Författarförlaget Fischer och Rye, Stockholm.
Elmér, Å., 1993, *Svensk socialpolitik,* Liber, Stockholm.
Eklund, K., 1981, 'Är Keynes verkligen död? Introduktion till den nya nationalekonomin', *Tiden* 7 pp. 503–513.
Eklund, K., 1982, *Den bistra sanningen. Om Sveriges ekonomi och de kommande magra åren.* Tidens debatt 6, Tiden, Stockholm.
Erlander, T., 1954, *Människor i samverkan,* Fakta och debatt 6.
Erlander, T., 1956, *Framstegens politik,* Tiden, Stockholm.
Erlander, T., 1962, *Valfrihetens samhälle,* Aktuellt 60–tal, Tidens Förlag, Stockholm.
Erlander, T., 1982, *Sextiotalet,* Tiden, Stockholm.
ESO, *Verksamhetsberättelse 1981/1982, 1982/1983, 1984/1985.*
Esping-Andersen, G., 1985, *Politics against markets. The social democratic road to power,* Princeton University Press, Princeton.
Esping-Andersen, G., 1990, *The three worlds of welfare capitalism,* Polity Press, Cambridge.
Esping-Andersen, G. and Korpi, W., 1987, 'From poor relief to institutional welfare states. The development of Scandinavian social policy', *International Journal of Sociology* 16, pp. 3–4.
Fairclough, N., 2000, *New Labour, new language,* Routledge, London.
Favretto, I., 2003, *The long search for a third way,* Palgrave Macmillan, London.
Feldt K.-O., 1980, 'Inför 1980–talet. Arbete, sparsamhet och hushållning', *Tiden* 1980 pp. 223–229.
Feldt K.-O., 1984, *Samtal med Feldt: Berndt Ahlqvist och Lars Engqvist intervjuar finansministern,* Tiden, Stockholm.
Feldt, K.-O., 1991, *Alla dessa dagar,* Norstedts, Stockholm.
Finansdepartementet, 1969, *Programbudgetering 1969. Redogörelse för försöksverk-*

samheten.
Finlayson, A., 2003, *Making sense of New Labour*, Lawrence and Wishart, London.
Florin, C. and Nilsson, B., 1999, 'Something in the nature of a bloodless revolution', in Torstendahl, R., ed., *State policy and the gender system in the two German states and Sweden 1945–1989*, Studia Historica Upsaliensia, Uppsala.
Foucault, M., 1972, *The archeology of knowledge*, Routledge, London.
Folkpartiet, 1959, *Världen och vi på 60–talet*, Stockholm.
Forskningsberedningen, 1968, *Samhällsforskning.*
Freire, P., 1972, *Pedagogik för förtryckta*, Gummesson, Stockholm.
Fridjonsdottir, K., 1991, 'Social science and the Swedish model. Sociology at the service of the welfare state', in Wagner, P., Wittrock, B. and Whitley, R., eds., *Discourses on society, the shaping of the social science disciplines*, Kluwer, Dordrecht.
Friman, E., 2002, *No limits. The 20th century discourse of economic growth*, Department of History, Umeå University, Umeå.
FSS (Föreningen Sveriges Socialchefer), 1966, *Serviceinriktad socialvård.*
FSS, 1967, *Sociallagstiftningen, hjälpmedel eller hinder.*
FSS, 1968, *Socialvården söker nya vägar.*
FSS, 1970, *Alternativ socialvård.*
FSS, 1971, *Socialvård i framtiden.*
FSS, 1972, *Ekonomi och välfärd.*
Friedman, M., 1977, *Välfärdsstatens myter: föredrag inför Företagsekonomiska och Nationalekonomiska föreningen i Skåne den 20 juni 1977*, Timbro, Stockholm.
Färm, G., 1991, *Carlsson – en samtalsbok med Ingvar Carlsson*, Tiden, Stockholm.
Galbraith, J.-K., 1958, *The affluent society*, Prisma, Stockholm.
Galbraith, J.-K., 1964, *Överflödets samhälle*. Prisma, Stockholm.
Gardiner, J., 1997, *Gender, care and economics*, Basingstoke, Macmillan.
Giddens, A., ed., 2001, *The global third way debate*, Polity Press, Cambridge.
Gough, I. and Olofsson, G., eds, 1999, *Capitalism and social cohesion. Essays on exclusion and integration*, Macmillan, London.
Hall, P.A., 1986, *Governing the economy. The politics of state intervention in Britain and France*, Oxford University Press, Oxford.
Hall, P.A., 1993, 'Policy paradigms, social learning, and the state. The case of economic policymaking in Britain', *Comparative Politics*, April 1993, pp. 275–296.
Hall, S., 1988, *Thatcherism and the crisis of the left. The hard road to renewal*, Verso, London.
Hall, S., 1996, 'The problem of ideology. Marxism without guarantees', in Hall, S., Morley, D., and Chen, K.-H., eds, *Critical dialogues in cultural studies*, Routledge, London /New York.
Hay, C., 1999, *The political economy of New Labour. Labouring under false pretences*, Manchester University Press, Manchester.
Hayek, F.A., 1983, *Frihetens grundvalar*, Ratio, Stockholm.
Harrington, M., 1962, *The other America. Poverty in the United States*, Macmillan, New York.
Haveman, R., 1987, *Poverty policy and poverty research: the great society and the social sciences*, University of Wisconsin Press, Madison Wisconsin.
Heclo, H. and Madsen, H., 1987, *Policy and politics in Sweden. Principled pragmatism*, Temple University Press, Philadelphia.
Hinnfors, J., 1992, *Familjepolitik*, Arkiv, Lund.
Hinnfors, J., 2005, 'Marketfriendly social democracy', paper to the second conference

Rethinking social democracy, Swansea, April 2005.
Hirdman, Y., 2000, *Att lägga livet till rätta*, Carlssons, Stockholm.
Holgersson, L., 1998, *Socialpolitik och socialt arbete*, Norstedts Juridik, Stockholm.
Holmberg, C., 1988, *Längtan till landet. Civilisationskritik och framstegsvisioner i 1970–talets regionalpolitiska debatt*, Department of History, Gothenburg University.
Holmberg, P., 1970, *Välstånd med slagsida*, Publica, Stockholm.
Holmberg, P., 1972, *Forskning om välfärden och dess fördelning i Sverige. Förslag till en vidareutveckling av Låginkomstutredningens arbete*, Ds In 1972:17, Stockholm.
Holmberg, B., 1986, *Nu våras det!* Civildepartementet, Stockholm.
Hugemark, A., 1994, *Den fängslande marknaden. Ekonomer om välfärdsstaten*, Arkiv, Lund.
Inghe, G., 1960, 'Utredning angående socialhjälpen i Stockholm', *Stadskollegiets utlåtanden och memorial* 86.
Inghe, G., 1960, *Fattiga i folkhemmet*, Tiden, Stockholm.
Inghe, G., 1967, *Den ofärdiga välfärden*, Tiden, Stockholm.
Jarl, S., 1968, *Dom kallar oss mods*, Aldus Bonnier, Stockholm.
Jarl, S., 1978, *Ett anständigt liv*, Norstedts, Stockholm.
Jessop, B., 2001, *The future of the welfare state*, Polity, Oxford.
Johansson, A.L., and Magnusson, L., 1998, *LO – andra halvseklet*, Atlas, Stockholm.
Johansson, S., 1970, *Om levnadsnivåundersökningen. Utkast till kapitel 1 och 2 i betänkande att avgivas av låginkomstutredningen*, Stockholm.
Johansson, S., 1979, *Mot en teori för social rapportering*, Institute for Social Research (SOFI), Stockholm.
Jonung, L., 1999, *Med backspegeln som kompass. Om stabiliseringspolitiken som läroprocess*, Ds 1999:9, Stockholm.
Karlsson, S., 2001, *Det intelligenta samhället. En omtolkning av socialdemokratins idéhistoria*, Carlssons, Stockholm.
Katz, M.B., 1989, *The undeserving poor. From President Johnson's war on poverty to Reagan's war on welfare*, Pantheon Books, New York.
Kommunalarbetareförbundet, 1980, *En helhetssyn på effektiviteten*, Stockholm.
Korpi, W., 1983, *The democratic class struggle*, Walter Kegan, London.
Korpi, W., 1985, *Marknad eller politik? Om de politiska alternativen i 1980–talets Sverige*, LO/Offentliga Samtal, Stockholm.
Kulawik, T., 1991, 'A productivist welfare state, the Swedish model revisited', in Borkowski T., ed., *Social policies in a time of transformation*, Goethe Institut and Jagellonian University, Krakow.
Kulawik, T., 2002, 'The Nordic Model of the Welfare State and the Trouble with a Critical Perspective', keynote lecture at the conference *Norden at the crossroads*, Helsinki, 30 October–2 November 2002.
Laclau, E. and Mouffe, C., 1985, *Hegemony and socialist strategy. Towards a radical democratic politics*, Verso, London.
Labour Party, 1997, *Because Britain deserves better*, London.
Lagergren, F., 1999, *På andra sidan välfärdsstaten*, Symposion, Stockholm.
Lewin, L., 1967, *Planhushållningsdebatten*, Tiden, Stockholm.
Levitas, R., 2005, *The inclusive society?*, Palgrave Macmillan, London.
Lindvall, J., 2004, *The politics of purpose. Macroeconomic policymaking in Sweden*, doctoral thesis, Department of Political Science, Gothenburg University, Gothenburg.
Lisbon European Council. *An agenda of economic and social renewal.*
LO, 1951, *Fackföreningsrörelsen och den fulla sysselsättningen.*

LO, 1961, *Samordnad näringspolitik. Strukturutredningen.*
LO, 1966, *Fackföreningsrörelsen och den tekniska utvecklingen.*
LO, 1971, *Låglön och välfärd. Rapport till LO:s lönepolitiska kommitté.*
LO, 1976, *Fackföreningsrörelsen och socialpolitiken. Socialpolitiska kommittén. Rapport till LO-kongressen 1976.*
LO, 1986, *Fackföreningsrörelsen och välfärdsstaten.*
LO-SAP, 1964, *Resultat och reformer.*
LO-SAP, 1972, *Näringspolitisk rapport.*
LO-SAP, 1973, *Sysselsättningspolitik för 70–talet.*
LO-SAP, 1978, *Sysselsättningspolitik inför 1980–talet.*
Lundberg, U. and Petersen, K., 1998, 'Velfaerdstatens fuldbyrdelse, krise og genkomst: socialdemokratiet i Danmark og Sverige fra 1960erne og frem', *Den Jytske historiker*, 82, pp. 92–114, Copenhagen.
Lundberg, U. and Åmark, K., 1997, 'En vänster i takt med tiden? 1960–talets politiska kultur i 1990–talets självförståelse', *Häften för kritiska studier* 2:1997, Stockholm.
Lundberg U., 2003, *Juvelen i kronan. Socialdemokraterna och den allmänna pensionen*, Hjalmarson och Högberg, Stockholm.
Lundberg, U., 2005, 'Social democracy lost. The social democratic party in Sweden and the politics of pension reform 1978–1998', working paper, Institute for Futures Studies, Stockholm.
Mann, K., 1999, 'Critical Reflections on the "Underclass" and Poverty', in Gough, I. and Olofsson, G., eds, *Capitalism and social cohesion. Essays on exclusion and integration*, Macmillan, London.
Marchand, M.H. and Runyan, A.S., 2000, *Gender and global restructuring*, Routledge, London.
McCloskey, D., 2001, *Measurement and meaning in economics. The essential Deirdre McCloskey*, Edward Elgar, New York.
Meidner, R., 1982, 'Den offentliga sektorns expansion', *Hotad sektor*, Stockholm.
Mellbourn, A., 1986, *Bortom det starka samhället. Socialdemokratin och den nya förvaltningspolitiken 1982–1986*, Carlsson, Stockholm.
Merkel, W., 2001, 'The third ways of social democracy', in Giddens, A., ed., *The global third way debate*, Polity Press, Cambridge.
Mishra, R., 1984, *The welfare state in crisis. Social thought and social change*, St Martins Press, New York.
Molina, I., 2000, *City template, multi-ethnic metropolitan Stockholm*, Partnership for multiethnic integration, Umeå.
Moschonas, G., 2002, *In the name of social democracy. The great transformation 1945 to the present*, Verso, London.
Moss, D.A., 1996, *Socializing security. Progressive era economists and the origins of American social policy*, Harvard University Press, Cambridge, MA.
Murhem, S., forthcoming, *'Security in change'. The Swedish concept of labour market flexibility.* Department of Economic History, Uppsala University.
Myrdal, G., 1932a, 'Socialpolitikens dilemma I', *Spektrum* 1, pp. 1–13.
Myrdal G., 1932b, 'Socialpolitikens dilemma II', *Spektrum* 2, pp. 12–31.
Myrdal G., 1932c, 'Kosta sociala reformer pengar?' *Arkitektur och samhälle*, 33, pp. 33–44.
NFS (Nordens fackliga samorganisation), 1980, *Fackföreningsrörelsen och den offentliga sektorn.*
O'Connor, A., 2001, *Poverty knowledge. Social science, social policy and the poor in twen-*

tieth-century U.S. history, Princeton University Press, Princeton.

OECD 1971, *Science, growth and society. Report of the Secretary General's ad hoc groups on new concepts in science policy*, Paris.

Offe, C., 1984, *Contradictions of the welfare state*, Studies in Contemporary German Thought, MIT Press, Cambridge, MA.

Olsson, S.E., 1990, *Social policy and welfare state in Sweden*, Arkiv, Lund.

Olsson, U., 1994, 'Planning in the Swedish welfare state', in Clemence, W. and Mahon R., eds, *Swedish social democracy. A model in transition*, Studies in Political Economy, Toronto.

Ortony, A., ed., 1993, *Metaphor and thought*, Cambridge University Press, Cambridge.

Östberg, K., 2002, 1968. *När allting var i rörelse. Sextiotalsradikaliseringen och de sociala rörelserna*, Prisma – Samtidshistoriska Perspektiv, Stockholm.

Palme, O., 1971, 'Tillväxt, balans, jämlikhet', *Vårt ekonomiska läge.*

Palme, O., 1972, 'Socialdemokratin i Europa starkare än någonsin', *Tiden*, 64 7/8 pp. 391–403.

Palme, O., 1977, *Med egna ord. Samtal med Serge Richard och Nordal Åkerman.* Brombergs Förlag, Uppsala.

Palme, O., 1987, *En levande vilja*, Tiden, Stockholm.

Palme, J., ed., 2002, *Welfare in Sweden, the balance sheet for the 1990s*, Ds 2002:32, Stockholm.

Palme, J., and Kangas, O., eds, 2005, *Social policy and economic development in the Nordic countries*, Palgrave Macmillan, Basingstoke.

Palme, J. and Wennemo, I., 1998, *Swedish social security in the 1990s. Reform and retrenchment*, Ministry of Social Affairs, Stockholm.

Persson, G., 1997, *Den som är satt i skuld är icke fri*, Atlas, Stockholm.

Pierson, P., ed., 2001, *The new politics of the welfare state*, Oxford University Press, Oxford.

Polanyi, K., 2001, *The great transformation. The political and economic origins of our time*, Beacon Press, Boston.

Pontusson, J., 1992, *The limits of social democracy Investment politics in Sweden*, Cornell, Ithaca.

Powell, M., ed., 1999, *New Labour, new welfare state? The third way in British social policy*, The Policy Press, London.

Regeringens proposition [government bill]1966:52, 1979/80:1.

Riksdagsmotion [parliamentary bills] 1978/79:600, 1978/79:2692, 1978/79:1124, 1979/80:1067, 1979/80:69, 1980/81:1136, 1980/81:71.

Riksdagens skrivelse (Parliamentary bill) 1958:78, 1956:176

Rodgers, D., 1998, *Atlantic crossings. Social politics in a progressive age*, Harvard University Press, Cambridge, MA.

Rothstein, B., 1985, 'Managing the welfare state. Lessons from Gustav Möller', *Scandinavian political studies*, vol. 8:3 pp. 151–170.

Rothstein, B., 1996, *The social democratic state. The Swedish social model and the bureaucratic problem of social reforms*, University of Pittsburgh Press, Pittsburgh.

Rothstein, B., 1998, *Just institutions matter*, Cambridge University Press, Cambridge, MA.

Rueschemeyer, D. and Skocpol, T., eds, 1996, *States, social knowledge and the origins of modern social policies*, Russell Sage Foundation/Princeton University Press, Princeton/New York.

Ruin, O., 1986, *I välfärdsstatens tjänst. Tage Erlander 1946–1969*, Tiden, Stockholm.

Runcis, M., 1998, *Steriliseringar i folkhemmet*, Ordfront, Stockholm.
Ryner, M., 2002, *Capitalist restructuring, globalisation and the third way. Lessons from the Swedish model*, Routledge Ripe Studies in Global Political Economy, London/New York.
Samuels, W.J., ed., 1990, *Economics as discourse*, Kluwer, Boston.
SAP, 1968, *Program för aktiv näringspolitik.*
SAP, 1969, *Jämlikhet, första rapport från arbetsgruppen för jämlikhetsfrågor.*
SAP, 1972a, *Jämlikhet, allas deltagande i arbetsliv och politik, andra rapporten från SAP:s och LO:s arbetsgrupp för jämlikhetsfrågor.*
SAP, 1972b, *Socialvård i utveckling. Rapport till socialdemokratiska partikongressen.*
SAP, 1974, *Välfärd och arbete åt alla.*
SAP, 1975a, *En demokratisk hushållning.*
SAP, 1975b, *Trygghet och rättvisa åt de handikappade, förslag till program för socialdemokratisk politik i handikappfrågor.*
SAP, 1975c, *Socialdemokratin och den unga generationen. Förslag till program för barns och ungdomars fritid.*
SAP, 1975d, *Partiprogram och kommunalt principprogram fastställda av 1975 års kongress.*
SAP, 1977, *Ekonomisk politik för 1980–talet.*
SAP, 1978, *Invandrarpolitiskt program. Jämlikhet, valfrihet, samverkan.*
SAP, 1979, *En social näringspolitik.*
SAP, 1981a, *Framtid för Sverige. Förslag till handlingslinjer för att föra Sverige ur krisen.*
SAP, 1981b, *Framtid för Sverige. Handlingslinjer för att föra Sverige ur krisen.*
SAP, 1983, *Kommunal socialpolitik.*
SAP, 1984a, *Framtiden i hela folkets händer.*
SAP, 1984b, *Slå vakt om solidariteten. Handikappolitiskt program.*
Socialdemokratiska ekonomgruppen 1981, *Solidaritet i de små och stora kollektiven: 11 uppsatser om organisatoriska strategier för den offentliga sektorn. Bommersviks seminarium om den offentliga sektorn*, Stockholm.
Socialdemokratiska ekonomgruppen 1982, *Nyliberalismen i praktiken.*
Sassoon, D., 1996, *One hundred years of socialism. The west European left in the 20th century*, IB Tauris, London.
Schön, D.A., 1993, 'Generative Metaphor, a Perspective on Problemsetting in Social Policy', in Ortony A., ed., *Metaphor and thought*, Cambridge University Press, Cambridge.
Schmidt, V.A., 2000, 'Values and discourse in the politics of adjustment', in Scharpf, F. and Schmidt, V.A., eds, *Work and welfare in the open economy*, Oxford University Press, Oxford.
Searle, J.R., 1995, *The construction of social reality*, Penguin, London.
Sejersted, F. 2005, *Socialdemokratins tidsålder. Sverige och Norge under 1900–talet*, Nya Doxa, Nora.
Skocpol, T. Rueschemeyer, D. and Evans P., eds, 1985, *Bringing the state back in*, Cambridge University Press, Cambridge.
Skocpol, T. and Weir, M., 1985, 'Institutional responses to the Great Depression in the United States, Britain and Sweden', in Skocpol, T., Rueschemeyer, D. and Evans P., eds, *Bringing the state back in*, Cambridge University Press, Cambridge.
Socialdemokraterna, 2001, *Partiprogram 2001.*
1959 års socialhjälpsundersökning (Investigation of benefits claimants 1959).
Socialstyrelsen 1968, *Ett principprogram om öppen vård*, Socialstyrelsen redovisar 1968:3.
Socialstyrelsen 1971, *Sociala mål, strukturförändringar, lösningar av relationsproblem i*

problemens miljö ger ett integrerat samhälle. Rapport från huvudgruppen för utredningen om den icke institutionsbundna socialvårdens målsättning och organisation. Socialstyrelsen redovisar 1971:21.

Socialstyrelsen 1972, *Sociala mål, social planering. Rapport från ett nordiskt seminarium för social planering 1971*, Socialstyrelsen redovisar 1972:27.

Sommestad, L., 1998, 'Human reproduction and the rise of welfare states. An economic-demographic approach to welfare state formation in the United States and Sweden', *Scandinavian Economic History Review*, 46:2, pp. 97–116.

Steinmetz, G., 1993, *Regulating the social. The welfare state and local politics in imperial Germany*, Princeton University Press, Princeton.

Stephens, J.D., 1979, *The Transition from capitalism to socialism*, New Studies in Sociology, London.

Stråth, B., 1998, *Mellan två fonder. LO och den svenska modellen*, Atlas, Stockholm.

SOU [*Statens offentliga utredningar*], 1956:53, *Balanserad expansion.*

SOU, 1961:29, *Socialförsäkringsutredningen.*

SOU, 1962:10, *Långtidsutredningen 1960.*

SOU, 1962:43, *Socionomutbildningskommittén.*

SOU, 1964:43, *Social omvårdnad av de handikappade.*

SOU, 1964:51, *Centrala rehabiliteringsberedningen.*

SOU, 1964:59, *Ett socialpolitiskt utredningsinstitut.*

SOU, 1965:9, *Arbetsmarknadsutredningen.*

SOU, 1965:13, *Långtidsutredningen 1965.*

SOU, 1965:49, *Hälso- och socialvårdens centrala organisation. Socialstyrelseutredningen.*

SOU, 1966:13, *Långtidsutredningen 1965, Socialvårdens utvecklingstendenser.*

SOU, 1966:45, *Aktiv åldringsvård och handikappvård.*

SOU, 1967:11, 1967:13, *Programbudgetutredningen.*

SOU, 1967:36, *Nykterhetsvårdens läge.*

SOU, 1970:34, *Svenska folkets inkomster.*

SOU, 1970:71, *Långtidsutredningen 1970.*

SOU, 1971:39, *Den svenska köpkraftsfördelningen 1967.*

SOU, 1973:43, *Budgetreform.*

SOU, 1974:39, *Socialvården. Socialutredningens principbetänkande.*

SOU, 1974:40, *Socialvården. Sammanfattning av Socialutredningens principbetänkande.*

SOU, 1975:89, *Långtidsutredningen 1975, Huvudrapport.*

SOU, 1975:90, 1978:14, *Sysselsättningsutredningens huvudbetänkande.*

SOU, 1977:40, *Socialtjänst och socialförsäkringstillägg. Lagar och motiv. Socialutredningens slutbetänkande.*

Spektorowski, A. and Mizrachi, E., 2004, 'Eugenics and the welfare state in Sweden. The politics of social margins and the idea of a productive society', *Journal of Contemporary History*, 39: 3, pp. 333–352.

Sundbom L., / Låginkomstutredningen 1970, *De extremt lågavlönade.*

Sundbom, L.,/ Låginkomstutredningen 1971, *De förvärvsarbetandes arbetsplatsförhållanden.*

SSU (Social Democratic Youth) 1967, *Inkomstklyftor och standardhöjning*, Prisma, Stockholm.

Taylor, R., 2005, *Sweden's new social democratic model. Proof that a better world is possible*, Compass, London.

Therborn, G., 1983, 'Brytningarnas och genombrottens årtionde. Den nya vänstern och resten av 60–talet', in Vikström, L., ed., *Marx i Sverige*, Arbetarkultur, Stockholm.

Tilton, T., 1990, *The political theory of Swedish social democrats. Through the welfare state to revolution*, Clarendon Press, Oxford.

Trägårdh, L., 2002a, 'Crisis and the politics of national community' in Witoszek, N. and Trägårdh, L., eds, *Culture and crisis. The case of Germany and Sweden*, Berghahn Books, New York.

Trägårdh, L., 2002b, 'Sweden and the EU. Welfare state nationalism and the spectre of Europe', in Hansen, L. and Waever, O., eds, *European integration and national identity. The challenge of the Nordic states*, Routledge, London, pp. 130–181.

Wagner, P., 1990, *Sozialwissenschaften und staat. Frankreich, Italien, Deutschland 1970–1980*, Campus Verlag, Frankfurt/New York.

Wagner, P., 2001, *A history and theory of the social sciences – not all that is solid melts into air*, Sage, New York.

Wagner, P., Wittrock, B. and Whitley, R., eds, 1991, *Discourses on society, the shaping of the social science disciplines*, Kluwer, Dordrecht.

Wagner, P., Weiss, P. and Wittrock, B., eds, 1991, *Social sciences and modern states, national experiences and theoretical crossroads*, Cambridge University Press, Cambridge.

Wennemo, I., 1992, 'Arbetarrörelsen och befolkningsfrågan. Knut Wicksell och makarna Myrdals befolkningsteorier', *Arkiv* 50 1991, pp. 61–73, Stockholm.

Williams, F., 2001, *Social policy, a critical introduction*, Polity, Cambridge.

Wigforss, E., 1932, *Har vi råd att arbeta. Något om sparsamhet och offentliga arbeten*, Tiden, Stockholm.

Zarefsky, D., 1986, *President Johnson's war on poverty. Rhetorics and history.* Alabama University Press, Alabama.

Archives

In the Labour movement's archives, *Arbetarrörelsens arkiv och bibliotek*, Stockholm:

Archives of the Crisis group, F 11 A, volumes 049.

Archives of the SDE, F 11 A, volumes 019, 020.

Archives of the Equality group, F 10 H, volumes 37, 38, 39.

SAP archives *rådslagsmaterial*, F 10 H, volumes 35, 36, 47, 48.

Sven Aspling's archives, volumes 'Fackliga och kongresstal 1963–75', 'Politiska tal 1964–69', 'Bakgrundsmaterial till Socialtjänsten och korrespondens med Samarbets-kommittén för socialvårdens målfrågor'.

Alva Myrdal's archives, *ämnesordnade, Jämlikhetsgruppen*, volumes 62–64d.

Ingvar Carlsson's archives, 2. 11, volumes 4, 5, 9.

Olof Palme's archives, 4. 2, volumes 54, 57, 147, 160, 161, 163, 170.

In the Swedish national archives, *Riksarkivet*, Stockholm:

Archives of the FSS [Föreningen Sveriges socialchefers arkiv] B, volumes 2, F, volume 2, 3.

Index